Crystallization-Study
of
Colossians

Volume One

The Holy Word for Morning Revival

Witness Lee

Living Stream Ministry
Anaheim, CA • www.lsm.org

First Edition, July 2004.

ISBN 0-7363-2612-X

Published by

Living Stream Ministry
2431 W. La Palma Ave., Anaheim, CA 92801 U.S.A.
P. O. Box 2121, Anaheim, CA 92814 U.S.A.

Printed in the United States of America

04 05 06 07 08 09 10 / 10 9 8 7 6 5 4 3 2 1

Contents

Preface

1. This book is intended as an aid to believers in developing a daily time of morning revival with the Lord in His word. At the same time, it provides a limited review of the Summer Training held June 28—July 3, 2004, in Anaheim, California, on the crystallization-study of Colossians. Through intimate contact with the Lord in His word, the believers can be constituted with life and truth and thereby equipped to prophesy in the meetings of the church unto the building up of the Body of Christ.

2. The entire content of this book is taken from the Crystallization-study Outlines: Colossians, the text and footnotes of the Recovery Version of the Bible, selections from the writings of Witness Lee and Watchman Nee, and *Hymns,* all of which are published by Living Stream Ministry.

3. The book is divided into weeks. One training message is covered per week. Each week presents first the message outline, followed by six daily portions, a hymn, and then some space for writing. The training outline has been divided into days, corresponding to the six daily portions. Each daily portion covers certain points and begins with a section entitled "Morning Nourishment." This section contains selected verses and a short reading that can provide rich spiritual nourishment through intimate fellowship with the Lord. The "Morning Nourishment" is followed by a section entitled "Today's Reading," a longer portion of ministry related to the day's main points. Each day's portion concludes with a short list of references for further reading and some space for the saints to make notes concerning their spiritual inspiration, enlightenment, and enjoyment to serve as a reminder of what they have received of the Lord that day.

4. The space provided at the end of each week is for composing a short prophecy. This prophecy can be composed by considering all of our daily notes, the "harvest" of our inspirations during the week, and preparing a main point

with some sub-points to be spoken in the church meetings for the organic building up of the Body of Christ.

5. Following the last week in this volume, we have provided a reading schedule for the New Testament Recovery Version with footnotes. This schedule is arranged so that one can read through the complete New Testament Recovery Version with footnotes in two years.

6. As a practical aid to the saints' feeding on the Word throughout the day, we have provided verse cards at the end of the volume, which correspond to each day's scripture reading. These may be cut out and carried along as a source of spiritual enlightenment and nourishment in the saints' daily lives.

7. The Crystallization-study Outlines were compiled by Living Stream Ministry from the writings of Witness Lee and Watchman Nee. The outlines, footnotes, and references in the Recovery Version of the Bible are by Witness Lee. All of the other references cited in this publication are from the published ministry of Witness Lee and Watchman Nee.

Summer Training
(June 28—July 3, 2004)

CRYSTALLIZATION-STUDY
OF COLOSSIANS

Banners:

The all-inclusive Christ,
the centrality and universality of God's economy,
is our life and the unique constituent
of the new man.

We need to walk in Christ as our living land
and absorb Christ as our rich soil
so that we may grow with the growth of God.

In His economy God gives us one person—
the all-inclusive, extensive, preeminent Christ—
and one way—the cross.

We need to allow the peace of Christ
to arbitrate in our hearts,
let the word of Christ dwell in us richly, and
persevere in prayer for the one new man.

Christ—the All-inclusive, Extensive, Preeminent One, the Centrality and Universality of God's Economy

Scripture Reading: Col. 1:9, 15-18, 27; 2:8, 16-17; 3:4, 10-11

Day 1   **I. The Christ unveiled in Colossians is the all-inclusive, extensive, preeminent One, the centrality and universality of God's economy (1:15-18, 27; 2:16-17; 3:4, 10-11):**

A. Colossians reveals the all-inclusive Christ—the One who is God, man, and the reality of every positive thing in the universe (2:9, 16-17).

B. For Christ to be the Firstborn of both the original creation and the new creation means that He is both all-inclusive and extensive (1:15, 18):

  1. The extensive Christ is the Christ who is more vast than the universe and who is everything to us (Eph. 3:18).

  2. Christ, the Savior in whom we believe, is limitless and inexhaustible; since He is without limitation, the revelation concerning Him must also be without limitation (vv. 2-5, 8).

C. Christ is the preeminent One, the One who has the first place in everything (Col. 1:18):

  1. Both in the old creation and the new creation, both in the universe and in the church, Christ occupies the first place, the place of preeminence (vv. 15, 18).

  2. If we have a vision of the preeminence of Christ, our living and our church life will be revolutionized, for we will realize that in all things Christ must have the first place (cf. Rev. 2:4).

Day 2   D. The all-inclusive, extensive Christ is the centrality and universality, the center and circumference, of God's economy (Col. 1:15-27; Eph. 1:10):

  1. In God's economy Christ is everything; God

wants Christ and Christ alone—the wonderful, preeminent, all-inclusive Christ, who is all and in all (Matt. 17:5; Col. 3:10-11).

2. The all-inclusive, extensive Christ is the center of God's economy; God's dispensing is altogether related to Christ and focused on Him (Eph. 3:17a).

3. God's intention in His economy is to work the wonderful, all-inclusive, extensive Christ into our being as our life and our everything that we may become the corporate expression of the Triune God (Col. 1:27; 3:4, 10-11).

Day 3 **II. The will of God is that the all-inclusive, extensive Christ be our portion (1:9, 12):**

A. In 1:9 God's will refers to Christ; the will of God is profound in relation to our knowing, experiencing, and living the all-inclusive, extensive Christ.

B. God's will is that we know Christ, experience Christ, enjoy Christ, be saturated with Christ, and have Christ become our life and person (3:4).

Day 4 **III. The all-inclusive, extensive Christ dwells in us as our hope of glory (1:27):**

A. We worship the enthroned Christ in the heavens, but we experience, enjoy, and partake of the indwelling Christ in our spirit; we are one with Him in a very subjective way (3:1; 1:27; 1 Cor. 6:17).

B. The Christ who indwells us is not a small, limited Christ but the all-inclusive, extensive Christ—the One who is the image of the invisible God, the Firstborn of all creation, the Head of the Body, and the embodiment of the fullness of God (Col. 1:15-16, 18-19).

Day 5 **IV. The all-inclusive, extensive Christ is our life (3:4):**

A. The expression *our life* is a strong indication that we are to experience the all-inclusive Christ, the One who is the reality of every positive thing (2:16-17).

B. The extensive Christ has become our life; universally, He is extensive, but in our personal experience, He is our life, our being.

C. Because Christ is our life, all He has and all He has attained and obtained become subjective to us (Rom. 8:34, 10).

V. **The all-inclusive, extensive Christ is the unique constituent of the one new man (Col. 3:10-11):**

A. The content of the church as the new man is Christ alone; in the new man there is room only for Christ, for He is everyone and in everyone.

B. In the church as the new man we are in Christ, through Christ, and unto Christ, and we subsist together in Christ to be God's expression in Christ (1:16-17).

C. God's ultimate goal in His economy is to gain the new man constituted with the all-inclusive, extensive Christ (Eph. 2:15; 4:24; Col. 3:10-11).

VI. **We should estimate and evaluate everything according to the all-inclusive, extensive Christ (2:8):**

A. Christ is the governing principle of all genuine wisdom and knowledge, the reality of all genuine teaching, and the only measure of all concepts acceptable to God.

B. Only when we have a clear view of the place of the all-inclusive, extensive Christ in God's economy will we be able to see through delusion and deception.

Day 6 VII. **We need to be infused, saturated, and permeated with the all-inclusive, extensive Christ until in our experience He is everything to us (1:27; 2:16-17; 3:4, 10-11):**

A. The all-inclusive, extensive Christ is in us, but we need to see Him, know Him, be filled with Him, be saturated with Him, and be absolutely one with Him.

B. We should allow the all-inclusive, extensive Christ to fill our whole being and to replace our culture with Himself (Eph. 3:17a; Col. 3:10-11):

1. The more Christ replaces our natural life

and culture with Himself, the more we will be able to declare, "To live is Christ"; to us to live will be the Christ who takes full possession of us, occupies us, and fills us with Himself (Phil. 1:21a).

2. The all-inclusive, extensive Christ desires to replace every element of our natural life and culture with Himself so that we may be the one new man as His corporate expression; this is the message of the book of Colossians.

Morning Nourishment

Col.   Who is the image of the invisible God, the Firstborn
1:15   of all creation.
  18   And He is the Head of the Body, the church; He is the
       beginning, the Firstborn from the dead, that He
       Himself might have the first place in all things.
Eph.   To me...was this grace given to announce to the Gen-
3:8   tiles the unsearchable riches of Christ as the gospel.

We need to see that Christ is the preeminent and all-inclusive
One, the centrality and universality of God. The book of
Colossians reveals that Christ is preeminent, that He has the
first place in everything. Both in the first creation and in the new
creation Christ occupies the first place. In 1:15 we are told that
Christ is the "Firstborn of all creation," and in 1:18, that He is the
"Firstborn from the dead." The new creation of God is by resurrection. For Christ to be preeminent in the new creation means that
He is the first in resurrection. He is the first both in creation and
in resurrection. This means that He is the first in the old creation,
the universe, and in the new creation, the church. The universe is
the environment in which the church exists as the Body of Christ
to express Christ in full. Christ is not only first in the church, the
Body, but also first in the environment, the universe. This means
that He is first in everything.

He is also the all-inclusive One. Christ is the reality of all the
positive things in the universe. If we know the Bible and God's
economy, we shall realize that Christ is the heavens, the earth, the
sun, life, light, the star, trees, flowers, water, air, and food. The mate-
rial things are pictures of what He is to us. Furthermore, Christ is
all the divine attributes, such as power, holiness, righteousness,
kindness, and love. He is also the human virtues, such as humility
and patience. Moreover, He is the church and every member of the
church, God's building, and every stone in the building. This means
that Christ is you and me. (*Life-study of Colossians,* pp. 41-43)

Today's Reading

In Colossians 1:18 Paul says, "That He Himself might have the first place in all things." In the Bible to be the first is to be all. Since Christ is the first both in the universe and in the church, He must be all things in the universe and the church. As the first, He is all.

God's way of reckoning in this matter is different from ours. According to our estimation, if Christ is the first, then something else should be the second, third, and others in sequence. However, from God's point of view, for Christ to be the first means that He is all.

The first Adam included not only Adam as an individual, but all of mankind. In the same principle, in the eyes of God, the first-born of the Egyptians included all the Egyptians. The firstborn includes all. Therefore, for Christ to be the Firstborn in the universe means that He is everything in the universe. In like manner, for Christ to be the Firstborn in resurrection means that He is everything in resurrection. For Christ to be the Firstborn both of the old creation and of the new creation means that He is everything both in the old creation and in the new creation. This corresponds to Paul's word in 3:11, where he says that in the new man, in the new creation, "...Christ is all and in all." In the new man Christ is everyone and in everyone. In the new creation there is room only for Christ.

We should not be held back by the narrow view of Christ held by many Christians. Christ is exceedingly extensive; He is unlimited. The Bible even speaks of "the unsearchable riches of Christ" (Eph. 3:8). Although Christ's riches are unsearchable, many Christians limit Him by their theology and teachings. They have only an elementary understanding of Him. Christ, the Savior in whom we believe, is not limited. He is inexhaustible, all-inclusive, limitless. No one can say how great He is. Since He is without limitation, the revelation concerning Him must also be without limit. In this matter the book of Colossians is crucial. Without this book, it would be difficult to realize that the revelation of Christ is unlimited and extensive. (*Life-study of Colossians,* pp. 74-75, 350)

Further Reading: Life-study of Colossians, msgs. 1, 5, 9-10, 34-35, 41, 48; *The Centrality and Universality of Christ,* ch. 1

Enlightenment and inspiration: _____

_____

_____

_____

Morning Nourishment

Matt. ...This is My Son, the Beloved, in whom I have found
17:5 My delight. Hear Him!

Gal. I am crucified with Christ; and *it is* no longer I *who*
2:20 live, but *it is* Christ *who* lives in me; and the *life* which
I now live in the flesh I live in faith, the *faith* of the Son
of God, who loved me and gave Himself up for me.

Eph. Unto the economy of the fullness of the times, to head
1:10 up all things in Christ...

3:17 That Christ may make His home in your hearts
through faith...

Col. To whom God willed to make known what are the
1:27 riches of the glory of this mystery among the Gentiles,
which is Christ in you, the hope of glory.

God's intention is to dispense Christ into us so that He may be our life and our everything. God wants Christ to be our righteousness, holiness, humility, and patience. Since Christ is everything, there is no need for us to decide to do anything or to be anything. Instead, we should simply turn to the Lord and say, "Lord, thank You. You are my life and my everything. You are the real God and the real man. When I need love, You are love. When I need humility, You, Lord, are humility. Whatever I need, You are."

God does not want us to try to be good husbands or wives, parents or children. God only wants one person—Christ. However, we should not preach this to our children prematurely. Instead, we should first preach to ourselves, telling ourselves that God does not want our self-improvement, but that He only wants Christ. He has dispensed Christ into us to be our life and our everything so that we may live Him and that He may dwell in us. There is no need for us to strive to be loving. Our love is limited. But Christ is love, unlimited love, and He lives in us. (*Life-study of Colossians,* pp. 324-325)

Today's Reading

God does not want us to try to be proper Christians—He only wants us to live Christ. We should forget about trying to be a good husband or wife and care only to live Christ. Let us love Him, contact Him, and be one with Him. How near and available He is! He is within us and is one spirit with us, waiting to be given the opportunity to live in us. If we would give Christ the ground to live in us, we should cease from all our efforts.

In the church meetings, we may enjoy singing, "Christ liveth in me, Christ liveth in me." However, when the meeting is over, we are the ones who live, not Christ. Instead of Christ living in us, our inward being is occupied with ourselves. But if we see the vision of Christ living in us, we shall stop all our doing. How blessed it is to do nothing and to let Christ live in us! The Lord does not want us to try to improve our behavior. He does not want us to try to be a good husband or wife. The Christian life is Christ living in us. In such a life, we and Christ have one life and one living. Christ lives in our living. Oh, we desperately need to see this vision! We need to pray, "Lord, show me the vision that God only wants one person. He wants Christ to live in me." This vision will spontaneously terminate all of our efforts and doings. It will turn us from our trying to the indwelling Christ.

The book of Colossians reveals that God wants Christ and Christ alone....God does not want anything of man's culture. God does not care for philosophy, religion, ordinances, observances, or any kind of "ism." God wants only the wonderful, preeminent, all-inclusive Christ, the One who is all in all. Although Christ is all-inclusive, He dwells in us as our life. As the indwelling One, He is waiting for the opportunity to live in us. He is living, real, practical, and available. On the one hand, on the throne He is the Lord of all; on the other hand, He is the life-giving Spirit in us. Both in the Christian life and in the church life, Christ is everything. (*Life-study of Colossians*, pp. 326-328)

Further Reading: Life-study of Colossians, msgs. 14, 21, 25, 28, 32, 37-38, 45-46, 50; *Elders' Training, Book 6: The Crucial Points of the Truth in Paul's Epistles*, ch. 7; *A General Sketch of the New Testament in the Light of Christ and the Church*, chs. 19-20

Enlightenment and inspiration: _____
_____
_____
_____

Morning Nourishment

Col. Therefore we also, since the day we heard of *it*, do not
1:9 cease praying and asking on your behalf that you
     may be filled with the full knowledge of His will in all
     spiritual wisdom and understanding.
12   Giving thanks to the Father, who has qualified you for
     a share of the allotted portion of the saints in the light.

We should not try in ourselves to do anything about the culture within us. What is of vital importance is that we see the vision of God's economy. God's economy is to work the living, all-inclusive person of Christ into us. According to the revelation in the book of Colossians, Christ is the portion of the saints, the Firstborn of all creation, the image of the invisible God, the Head of the Body, the Firstborn from the dead, the One in whom all the fullness is pleased to dwell, the mystery of God's economy, the mystery of God, the reality of all positive things, and the constituent of the new man. Christ is everything: He is life, light, power, might, strength, righteousness, holiness, kindness, and every other divine attribute and human virtue. Because Christ is everything to us, He is all-inclusive. God's intention in His economy is to work this all-inclusive One into us. As the all-inclusive One, Christ has the highest attainments. He has ascended to the heavens and has been exalted to the highest place in the universe. He is now sitting at the right hand of God. Christ has been enthroned, and He has become the Lord and Head over all. Furthermore, He has obtained everything, for all things have become His. This person with all He has attained and obtained is the very One that God desires to work into our being. (*Life-study of Colossians,* pp. 330-331)

Today's Reading

God's will in [Colossians 1:9] refers to the will of His eternal purpose, of His economy concerning Christ (Eph. 1:5, 9, 11), not His will in minor things.

Years ago, when young saints asked about things such as

marriage or employment, I referred them to this verse in Colossians. I told them that they should seek spiritual knowledge in order to know God's will. But the will of God here is not focused on things such as marriage, jobs, or housing; it is concerned with the all-inclusive Christ as our portion. The will of God for us is that we know the all-inclusive Christ, experience Him, and live Him as our life. To know Christ in this way is to have the full knowledge of God's will.

The will of God is profound in relation to our knowing, experiencing, and living the all-inclusive Christ. In verse 9 Paul was not praying that the Colossians would know whom to marry, where to live, or what kind of job they should have. His heart was not occupied with such trivial things. In this verse God's will refers to Christ. It was not God's will for the Colossians to follow Judaistic observances, Gentile ordinances, or human philosophies. Furthermore, it was not God's will for them to practice asceticism, to treat the body severely in order to bridle the indulgence of the flesh. God's will for the Colossians was to know Christ, to experience Christ, to enjoy Christ, to live Christ, and to have Christ become their life and their person. God's will for us today is exactly the same. It seems as if Paul was saying, "Colossians, you have been distracted, misled, and defrauded by Gnosticism, mysticism, asceticism, observances, and ordinances. You need to be filled with the full knowledge of God's will. God's will is that the all-inclusive Christ be your portion."

If we know that God's will is for us to be saturated with Christ, then we have the proper knowledge of God's will. Whatever we do should be done in the will of God. We should marry in Christ, work in Christ, and move in Christ. Christ should be our life and our person. This is the will of God. (*Life-study of Colossians,* pp. 19-21)

Further Reading: Life-study of Colossians, msgs. 3, 39; *A General Sketch of the New Testament in the Light of Christ and the Church,* chs. 19-20

Enlightenment and inspiration: _____

_____

_____

_____

Morning Nourishment

Col. If therefore you were raised together with Christ,
3:1 seek the things which are above, where Christ is,
sitting at the right hand of God.

1:27 To whom God willed to make known what are the
riches of the glory of this mystery among the Gentiles, which is Christ in you, the hope of glory.

1 Cor. But he who is joined to the Lord is one spirit.
6:17

I believe that the time is right for messages on Christ versus culture to be released. It is vital for us all to see a vision
concerning the all-inclusiveness of Christ. Christ must become everything to us in our daily living. The Christ who is
the expression of God and the mystery of God's economy now
lives in us. The Christ who indwells us is not a small, limited
Christ. He is the One who is the image of the invisible God, the
embodiment of the fullness of God, and the focal point of God's
economy. Such a Christ now dwells in us and is waiting for the
opportunity to spread Himself throughout our being. We need
to live by Him moment by moment. We should not give any
ground in our living to culture. Instead, all the room within us
should be given over to the all-inclusive Christ who dwells in
us to be our hope of glory. If we see such a vision of the indwelling, all-inclusive Christ, we shall spontaneously drop our culture. Formerly, Christ was replaced by culture. But once we
see this vision, the culture within us will be replaced by
Christ. (*Life-study of Colossians,* p. 309)

Today's Reading

Many readers of the New Testament consider Colossians a
book of doctrine. However, Colossians is also a book of experience. The extensive, all-inclusive Christ revealed in this book
is subjective to us, for He dwells in us as our hope of glory
(1:27), and He is our life (3:4). Nothing can be more subjective
to us than our own life. In fact, our life is us. To say that Christ
is our life means that Christ becomes us. How could Christ be
our life without actually becoming us? It would be impossible.

He becomes us in our experience. As Paul says, "To me, to live is Christ" (Phil. 1:21). We have pointed out that Christ cannot be our life without becoming us. Life is our very being. Hence, for Christ to be our life means that He becomes our being. For Christ to become our being is for Christ to become us.

To us, Christ is both objective and subjective. We know Christ both according to doctrine and according to experience. On the one hand, our Christ is on the throne in the heavens. On the other hand, He is in our spirit. We worship the enthroned Christ in the heavens, but we experience, enjoy, and partake of the indwelling Christ in our spirit. We are one with Him in a very subjective way. As Paul says in 1 Corinthians 6:17, "He who is joined to the Lord is one spirit." Christ is subjective to us to such a degree that He and we, we and He, have become one spirit. To be one spirit with the Lord is greater than to have gifts and miracles. Now that we have become one spirit with the Lord, in our daily life we need to experience being one spirit with Him.

Some years ago I stayed with some saints who talked a lot about Colossians 1:27. Although they could speak of the indwelling Christ as the hope of glory, they had very little experience of Christ. To them, the indwelling Christ was merely a doctrine, not a reality. In their practical daily living, they were ethical and religious, but they did not live Christ. Even their love was a natural, ethical love, not the expression of Christ lived out from within them. In these believers you could see religion and ethics, but you could not see much of Christ. This is true of many Christians today. They know Christ in doctrine, but they have very little genuine experience of Him. However, when Paul wrote the book of Colossians, he wrote both according to doctrine and according to experience. (*Life-study of Colossians,* pp. 443-444)

Further Reading: Life-study of Colossians, msgs. 36, 51; *The Indwelling Christ in the Canons of the New Testament,* ch. 16

Enlightenment and inspiration: _____

_____

_____

_____

Morning Nourishment

Col. When Christ our life is manifested, then you also will
3:4 be manifested with Him in glory.
10-11 And have put on the new man, which is being renewed
unto full knowledge according to the image of Him
who created him, where there cannot be Greek and
Jew, circumcision and uncircumcision, barbarian,
Scythian, slave, free man, but Christ is all and in all.

The book of Colossians reveals that in God's economy Christ
is everything....Eventually, this preeminent, all-inclusive
Christ is the unique constituent of the new man. Furthermore,
as Paul declares in 3:4, this Christ is our life. The expression "our
life" is a strong indication that we are to experience in our daily
living the Christ revealed in this book.

For our physical existence, everything depends on our having
life....Everything associated with the human living is based on
having human life. If the life is terminated, everything else is terminated also. This underscores the importance of Christ being
our life. It is vital for us to see that the all-inclusive Christ is our
life, [and that]...this Christ has been processed to become the
all-inclusive life-giving Spirit. (*Life-study of Colossians*, p. 276)

Today's Reading

Another aspect is found in Colossians 2:16 and 17, where
Paul says that eating, drinking, feasts, new moons, and Sab-
baths are "a shadow of things to come, but the body is of Christ."
Paul's word indicates that Christ is the reality of all positive
things. He is our real food, drink, clothing, dwelling place, trans-
portation, sun, moon, and earth. Hence, Paul's simple word in
these verses...implies the extensiveness of the all-inclusive Christ.

Then in 3:4 Paul goes on to tell us that this extensive Christ
is our life. Although Christ is universally extensive, He is nonetheless our life in a specific and particular way. Praise the Lord
that the extensive Christ has become our personal life! Universally,
He is extensive. But in our personal experience, He is our life.

Furthermore, in 3:10 and 11 we see that in the church, the

new man as God's new creation, the extensive Christ, is all and in all. He is all the members of the new man, and He is in all the members....[Hence], Christ is all of us. What an extensive, all-inclusive Christ is revealed in the book of Colossians!

Today I can testify that, through the Lord's grace, I no longer try to suppress myself. I simply live Christ. As Paul said, "To me, to live is Christ" (Phil. 1:21). Christ is my culture, my goal, and the meaning and purpose of my human life. In my daily walk all the room is for Christ. For this reason, there is no room for sin, the world, the flesh, or the self. Since my whole being is for Christ, there is also no room for culture. I simply live Christ, and not a limited Christ, but an extensive Christ, the One who fills all and is in all.

Christ descended from the heavens to the earth and then, in the interval between His death and resurrection, He descended into Hades. In resurrection He ascended from Hades to earth and then, in His ascension, from the earth to the heavens. As a result of such a universal traveling, Christ fills all things. Thus, He is the extensive One. As such an extensive One, He is our life, and we may live Him. In the book of Colossians Paul presents such an extensive Christ in order to impress us with the fact that this Christ should replace our culture. Do not try to drop your culture. All your efforts to do so will be in vain. Simply live Christ, and Christ will replace your culture with Himself.

We should not treasure any type of "ism," for all "isms" have to do with culture. Instead of living according to an ism, we should live Christ, a living person, who is the portion of the saints, the image of the invisible God, the Firstborn of both the old creation and the new creation, the One in whom and unto whom all things were created, and the One who is our life in the new man. Such an extensive Christ is the replacement for our culture. (*Life-study of Colossians,* pp. 389, 394)

Further Reading: Life-study of Colossians, msgs. 21, 30, 33, 35-36, 39, 45, 50, 53-54

Enlightenment and inspiration: _____

_____

_____

Morning Nourishment

Eph. **That Christ may make His home in your hearts**
3:17 **through faith...**
Phil. **For to me, to live is Christ...**
1:21

This Christ is the image of God, the full expression of God. He is not the hidden God, the concealed, mysterious God; He is God expressed, the image of the invisible God. Furthermore, He is the first among God's creation. As we have pointed out, this indicates that He is everything. He is the Alpha, the Omega, and all the letters in between (Rev. 22:13). He is everything in the universe, and He is the first in the new creation, the church.

Perhaps you are wondering how this understanding of Christ can help you in a practical way. If for a period of thirty days you are occupied with the revelation of Christ in Colossians, you will be revolutionized, reconstituted, and transformed. Pray over these messages on Colossians and have fellowship concerning them, and you will see what a difference it will make in you. I can testify that it makes a tremendous difference when the vision of the all-inclusiveness of Christ pervades our being. When you see this vision, you will hate everything that issues from the self. You will despise not only your hatred, but even your love, kindness, and patience. As this vision causes you to hate the self, it will constrain you to love the Lord. You will say, "Lord Jesus, I love You because You are everything. Lord, there is no need for me to struggle or strive to do anything. O Lord, You are so much to me. You are God, You are the Firstborn of all creation, and You are the Firstborn from among the dead." I suggest that you pray-read Colossians for thirty days. Pray until all the aspects of Christ revealed in this book saturate your being. We do not need regulations or teachings—we need to be infused and saturated with Christ as the all-inclusive One. (*Life-study of Colossians,* pp. 76-77)

Today's Reading

If Christ is infused into you, you will drop everything that is not Christ, and you will be constituted with Christ in your very being. Religion gives people doctrines and teaches them how to behave. The book of Colossians, on the contrary, speaks of the all-inclusive Christ. This Christ is already in us, but we need to see Him, know Him, be filled with Him, be saturated with Him, and become absolutely one with Him.

However, if we would keep from paying attention to the self, we must concentrate on something better than the self. This is the reason we need a vision of the extensiveness of Christ, the vision presented in the book of Colossians. If we see this vision, we shall concentrate our entire being on the extensive Christ, who will then fill us and occupy us. Because we are filled with the extensive Christ, we shall have no need of Judaism, Gnosticism, mysticism, or asceticism. Our being will be occupied with the vast, unsearchably rich, extensive Christ. Spontaneously this Christ will come in to replace every aspect of our natural human life with Himself.

The book of Colossians presents a vision of the wonderful, extensive, all-inclusive Christ. Once we see this vision, our entire being will be attracted by this Christ and will be possessed by Christ and occupied with Him. Then gradually the extensive Christ who occupies our attention will replace every element of our natural human life. He will even replace with Himself our kindness, our humility, and our love for our parents. At best, our natural virtues can be compared to polished copper, but Christ is gold. He far surpasses in value anything we possess by nature. The more we experience the Christ who exceeds everything and replaces everything in our natural life with Himself, the more we shall be able to declare, "To me, to live is Christ." We shall not live humility, kindness, or patience. To us to live will be the Christ who has taken full possession of us and who occupies us and fills us with Himself. That such a Christ should replace all the elements of our natural human life is the message of the book of Colossians. If we understand this underlying concept, Colossians will be an open book to us. (*Life-study of Colossians,* pp. 77, 428-429)

Further Reading: Life-study of Colossians, msgs. 9, 49

Enlightenment and inspiration: _____

_____

_____

_____

Hymns, #495

1   Christ is God's centrality
    And His universality;
    He is God's delight and joy
    Throughout all eternity.

2   He's th' embodiment of God,
    In Him all God's fulness dwells;
    His unique supremacy
    And His Godhead none excels.

3   All God's purpose is for Him,
    That He might be all in all;
    All the things in heav'n and earth
    With Himself are made withal.

4   All creation is for Christ,
    Everything was made by Him;
    'Tis by Him all things subsist,
    He's the hub and He's the rim.

5   In redemption He is all,
    All through Him is reconciled;
    By His blood all things with God
    Now in peace are domiciled.

6   He the great beginning is,
    And the Church's living Head;
    He her life and content too,
    And the firstborn from the dead.

7   In God's Kingdom He's the King,
    All the pow'r to Him is giv'n;
    In His glory He shall rule
    Over all in earth and heav'n.

8   In new heaven and new earth
    Center of all things He'll be,
    For the Godhead and for man
    Throughout all eternity.

9   God intends in everything
    Christ should have preeminence,
    And that such a Christ of all
    We should now experience.

Composition for prophecy with main point and sub-points: _____

_____

_____

_____

_____

_____

_____

_____

_____

_____

_____

_____

_____

_____

_____

_____

_____

_____

_____

_____

_____

_____

_____

_____

_____

_____

_____

_____

_____

_____

_____

_____

_____

_____

_____

_____

_____

Enjoying the All-inclusive Christ as the Good Land—Our Allotted Portion

Scripture Reading: Col. 1:12; 2:6-15, 19; Exo. 3:8; Deut. 8:8-9; 26:9

Day 1   I. **Christ as the preeminent and all-inclusive One is the allotted portion of the saints (Col. 1:12):**

A. The allotted portion refers to the lot of the inheritance, as illustrated by the allotment of the good land of Canaan given to the children of Israel for their inheritance (Josh. 14:1).

B. The New Testament believers' allotted portion is not a physical land; it is the all-inclusive Christ as the life-giving Spirit (Col. 2:6-7; Gal. 3:14):

1. The riches of the good land typify the unsearchable riches of Christ in different aspects as the bountiful supply to His believers in His Spirit (Deut. 8:7-10; Eph. 3:8; Phil. 1:19).

2. By enjoying the riches of the land, the believers in Christ are built up to be His Body as the house of God and the kingdom of God (Eph. 1:22-23; 2:21-22; 1 Tim. 3:15; Matt. 16:18-19; Rom. 14:17).

Day 2   II. **The purpose of God's calling is to bring God's chosen people into the enjoyment of the all-inclusive Christ, typified by the good land flowing with milk and honey (Exo. 3:8; cf. 1 Cor. 1:9):**

A. Milk and honey, which are the mingling of both the animal life and the vegetable life, are two aspects of the life of Christ—the redeeming aspect and the generating aspect (Deut. 8:8; 26:9; cf. John 1:29; 12:24):

1. The redeeming aspect of Christ's life is for our judicial redemption, and the generating aspect of Christ's life is for our organic salvation (1:29; 12:24; Rev. 2:7; Rom. 5:10).

2. The symbols of the Lord's table signify the redeeming and generating aspects of Christ's life for God's complete salvation; thus, the good land has become a table, a feast for our enjoyment (Matt. 26:26-28; 1 Cor. 10:16-17).

B. We must be *in the light* in order to enjoy the all-inclusive Christ as the good land in His redeeming and generating aspects (Col. 1:12; 1 Pet. 2:9; Isa. 2:5):
   1. God is light (1 John 1:5).
   2. The word of God is light (Psa. 119:105, 130).
   3. Christ is light (John 8:12; 9:5).
   4. The life of Christ is light (1:4).
   5. The believers are light (Matt. 5:14; Phil. 2:15).
   6. The church is a lampstand shining with light (Rev. 1:20; Psa. 73:16-17).

Day 3

C. We must eat God's words to enjoy the all-inclusive Christ as the good land in His redeeming and generating aspects; God's word is milk for us to drink and honey for us to eat (John 6:57, 63, 68; 1 Pet. 2:2; Psa. 119:103; Ezek. 3:3).

D. By enjoying Christ as the land of milk and honey, we will be constituted with Him as milk and honey—"Your lips drip fresh honey, my bride; / Honey and milk are under your tongue" (S. S. 4:11a):
   1. Honey restores the stricken ones, whereas milk feeds the new ones.
   2. The seeker has stored so many riches within her that food is under her tongue, and she can dispense the riches of Christ to the needy ones at any time (Isa. 50:4; Luke 4:22; Eph. 4:29-30; cf. Matt. 12:35-36).
   3. This sweetness is not produced overnight, but comes from a long period of gathering, inward activity, and careful storage (S. S. 4:16; 2 Cor. 12:7-9).

Day 4   III. **We can walk in Christ as our living land and**
&   **absorb Christ as our rich soil, in which we**
Day 5   **have been rooted, so that we may grow with**
                 the elements that we absorb from the soil
                 (Col. 2:6-7; cf. 1 Cor. 3:6, 9; Col. 2:19):

A. Colossians 2:8-15 presents a full description
   and definition of Christ as the soil, in which we
   do not lack anything; as we take time to absorb
   Him as the all-inclusive land, the facts in these
   verses become our experience:

1. Christ as the soil is the One in whom all the
   fullness of the Godhead dwells bodily (v. 9):

   a. *Fullness* refers not to the riches of God
      but to the expression of the riches of God;
      what dwells in Christ is not only the
      riches of the Godhead but the expression
      of the riches of what God is (v. 9; 1:15, 19;
      3:10-11).

   b. When we are rooted in Christ as the soil,
      we are made full in Him; we are filled up
      with all the divine riches to become His
      expression (Eph. 3:8, 17, 19).

   c. In Christ as the soil we are filled, com-
      pleted, perfected, satisfied, and thor-
      oughly supplied; we do not lack anything
      (cf. Phil. 1:19).

   d. Christ as the soil is the history and mys-
      tery of God with all the riches of His per-
      son and processes (Col. 2:2).

2. Christ as the soil is the Head of all rule and
   authority (v. 10).

3. In Christ as the soil there is the killing
   power, which puts the flesh to death (v. 11).

4. In Christ as the soil there is an element
   which causes us to be buried (v. 12a).

5. In Christ as the soil there is an element
   which causes us to be raised up (v. 12b).

6. In Christ as the soil there is an element
   which vivifies us (v. 13).

7. In Christ as the soil there is the wiping out of the handwriting in ordinances (v. 14).

8. In Christ as the soil there is the victory over the evil spirits in the atmosphere (v. 15).

Day 6   B. We must take time to enjoy the Lord as the all-inclusive land so that all the elements of Christ as the rich soil may be absorbed into us for us to be made full in Him in our experience (v. 10a; 4:2):

1. If we would absorb the riches of Christ as the soil, we need to have tender, new roots (cf. 2 Cor. 4:16).

2. We need to forget our situation, our condition, our failures, and our weaknesses and simply take time to absorb the Lord; as we take time to absorb Him, we grow with the growth of God in us for the building up of the Body of Christ (Matt. 14:22-23; 6:6; Col. 2:7a, 19b; cf. Luke 8:13).

Morning Nourishment

Col.
1:12
Giving thanks to the Father, who has qualified you for a share of the allotted portion of the saints in the light.

2:6-7
As therefore you have received the Christ, Jesus the Lord, walk in Him, having been rooted and being built up in Him, and being established in the faith even as you were taught, abounding in thanksgiving.

Gal.
3:14
In order that the blessing of Abraham might come to the Gentiles in Christ Jesus, that we might receive the promise of the Spirit through faith.

God's promise to Abraham with respect to the good land is of great significance. When Paul was writing the Epistle to the Colossians and was speaking of the allotted portion of the saints, he no doubt had in mind the picture of the allotting of the good land to the children of Israel in the Old Testament....God gave His chosen people, the children of Israel, the good land for their inheritance and enjoyment. The land meant everything to them.

Christ is our portion, our lot, our everything, just as the land was all things to the children of Israel. The land provided whatever the children of Israel needed: milk, honey, water, cattle, grain, minerals. In writing this Epistle, Paul employed the concept of the all-inclusive land in order to charge the misled Colossians not to take anything other than Christ Himself. Anything that is not Christ is related to the authority of darkness, and we should not accept it. Rather, we should simply remain in the good land and not allow any foreign element to come in. Christ alone is our portion, and we should accept only what is of Him. (*Life-study of Colossians,* pp. 48-49)

Today's Reading

We need to be deeply impressed that this good land typifies the all-inclusive Christ. We have pointed out that in Colossians 2:7 Paul says that we have been rooted in Christ. If we have been rooted in Christ, then He must be our soil, our earth. Have you ever realized that Christ is the very land in which you are rooted, that you are a plant rooted in Christ as the soil? I deeply feel that most of the Lord's children are still in Egypt. They have experienced the Lord only as the Passover Lamb. Others have come out of Egypt and enjoy Christ as their daily manna as they wander in the wilderness. But very few believers experience Christ as the realm, the sphere, in which they walk. May the Lord open our eyes to see that Christ is our good land and that we must daily walk in Him!

In Galatians 3:14…Paul refers to the blessing of Abraham and the promise of the Spirit. This blessing refers to the good land, and the fulfillment of this blessing for us today is Christ as the all-inclusive Spirit. Therefore, according to Paul's concept, to walk in Christ as the good land is to walk in the all-inclusive Spirit.

In Colossians 2:6 Paul tells us to walk in Christ, but in Galatians 5:16 he charges us to walk by the Spirit. Furthermore, in Romans 8:4 he speaks of walking according to the spirit. These verses indicate that the good land for us today is the all-inclusive Spirit who indwells our spirit. This all-inclusive Spirit is the all-inclusive Christ as the processed Triune God. After being processed, the Triune God is the all-inclusive Christ as the all-inclusive Spirit for us to experience. Today this all-inclusive Spirit indwells our spirit to be our good land.

Christ today is the all-inclusive Spirit. Christ is the embodiment of God and the expression of God. Through incarnation, He became the last Adam, who was crucified on the cross for our redemption. In resurrection this last Adam became a life-giving Spirit (1 Cor. 15:45). Therefore, in 2 Corinthians 3:17 Paul says, "And the Lord is the Spirit." Because Christ as the life-giving Spirit dwells in our spirit, we are one spirit with Him. In 2 Timothy 4:22 Paul says, "The Lord be with your spirit," and in 1 Corinthians 6:17, "He who is joined to the Lord is one spirit." Therefore, Christ as the all-inclusive good land is now in our spirit. (*Life-study of Colossians,* pp. 167-168)

Further Reading: Life-study of Colossians, msgs. 6, 20; *Life-study of 1 Corinthians,* msg. 50; *Christ—Our Portion,* ch. 1

Enlightenment and inspiration: _____

_____

_____

_____

Morning Nourishment

Psa. Your word is a lamp to my feet and a light to my
119:105 path.

Phil. That you may be blameless and guileless, children
2:15 of God without blemish in the midst of a crooked
and perverted generation, among whom you shine
as luminaries in the world.

1 Pet. But you are a chosen race, a royal priesthood, a holy
2:9 nation, a people acquired for a possession, so that
you may tell out the virtues of Him who has called
you out of darkness into His marvelous light.

1 John ...God is light and in Him is no darkness at all.
1:5

Colossians 1:12 indicates that we partake of Christ as the
portion of the saints in the light. Since God alone is light, we
must turn to God and be in His presence in order to partake of
Christ. We have been called into the marvelous light of God
(1 Pet. 2:9). Before we were saved, we were altogether in darkness. Everything related to us and our human situation was in
darkness. When the gospel came to us, it came with light. This
caused us to repent to God. As we repented, we spontaneously
opened to Him. At the time we repented and were saved, we experienced something shining within us. We believed in the Lord
Jesus and thanked Him for dying on our behalf, and we received
Him as our Savior and Lord. In this way, the inner shining was
intensified. Therefore, at the time of our conversion, light entered into us. Many of us can testify that in the days following
our conversion we experienced such a light. In that light Christ
became our portion. (*Life-study of Colossians,* p. 58)

Today's Reading

The only way to partake of Christ and to enjoy Him is in
the light. God and Christ are light. When we turn to the Lord
and come into His presence, we are in the light and spontaneously begin to enjoy Him as our portion.

All Christians should read the Bible. However, it is possible to be in darkness even when we are reading the holy Word.

We may read the Scriptures without being in the presence of the Lord. If we do this, the more we study the Bible, the more we shall be in darkness, removed from the Lord's presence. The proper way to read the Scriptures is not only with the mind, but also with our seeking spirit, looking to the Lord's countenance as we read....When we read the Bible in a pray-reading spirit, opening ourselves to the Lord, we are brought into His presence. Spontaneously we are in the light, and Christ becomes our portion.

Because I have found that arguing puts me in darkness, I cannot bear to argue. Time after time, I am forced to stop speaking because of the threat of darkness. I pray to the Lord and ask Him to forgive me for expressing the self. Through such repentance and confession the light returns and I am able to continue to enjoy Christ.

Light is the presence of God. If we would be in light, we must turn to Him from within. Then His presence will become the shining light. In this way Christ becomes the portion of the saints in a practical way.

We need to have more and more contact with the Lord. We need to read His Word with an unveiled face and an open heart. As we fellowship with the Lord and follow the inner anointing, we shall experience Him as the life within us in a practical way. This life is the light. If we follow the inner anointing, we shall be in light. We are also brought into the light by fellowshipping with others in a genuine way. In fellowship there is the shining of light. Moreover, we need to be in the church life and attend the meetings, for in the church and in the meetings we are in the light. In the meetings of the church we often have the sense deep within that we are in the light enjoying Christ as our portion. All these are means by which we may be in the light to enjoy Christ as the portion of the saints. (*Life-study of Colossians,* pp. 59-61)

Further Reading: Life-study of Colossians, msg. 7

Enlightenment and inspiration: _____

_____

_____

Morning Nourishment

S. S. Your lips drip fresh honey, *my* bride; honey and
4:11 milk are under your tongue...

Psa. How sweet are Your words to my taste! Sweeter
119:103 than honey to my mouth!

Isa. The Lord Jehovah has given me the tongue of the
50:4 instructed, that I should know how to sustain the
weary with a word....

Luke And all bore witness to Him and marveled at the
4:22 words of grace proceeding out of His mouth...

Eph. Let no corrupt word proceed out of your mouth, but
4:29 only that which is good for building up, according to
the need, that it may give grace to those who hear.

The purpose of God's calling is a matter of tremendous signif-icance. In typology, bringing the children of Israel into the good land signifies bringing people into Christ, the all-inclusive per-son typified by the land of Canaan. Christ today is a good land flowing with milk and honey.

In His wisdom God uses the expression "flowing with milk and honey" to describe the riches of the good land. Both milk and honey are products of a combination of the vegetable life and the animal life. Milk comes from cattle, which feed on grass. The ani-mal life produces milk from the supply of the vegetable life. Therefore, milk is a product of the mingling of two kinds of life. The principle is the same with honey. Honey has much to do with the plant life. It is derived mostly from flowers and trees. Of course, a part of the animal life is also involved—that little ani-mal, the bee. Hence, in the production of honey, two kinds of life cooperate. These two kinds of life are mingled together, and honey is produced. (*Life-study of Exodus,* p. 62)

Today's Reading

Milk and honey signify the riches of Christ, riches that come from the two aspects of the life of Christ. Although Christ is one person, He has the redeeming life, typified by the animal life, and the generating life, typified by the vegetable life. On the one hand, Christ is the Lamb of God to redeem us; on the other hand, He is a loaf of barley to supply us. Both kinds of life were part of the passover meal, for in the passover there were the lamb and the unleavened bread with bitter herbs. These lives were combined for the enjoyment of God's redeemed people. The purpose of God's calling, however, is not to give His people a little enjoyment of the animal life and the vegetable life in Egypt; it is to bring them into a spacious land flowing with milk and honey. Do you have the assurance that in the church life today you are enjoying Christ as the good land? I can testify that I daily enjoy Christ as a spacious land flowing with milk and honey. (*Life-study of Exodus,* pp. 62-63)

[In Song of Songs 4:11], from the mouth of the maiden issue forth sweet and refreshing words, not gossip, jokes, or rash words. Her words are not outbursts of torrents, but drops of honey from the honeycomb. This is the slowest kind of dripping. Some people have the urge to speak; their words are like the babbling of brooks. Even when they speak about spiritual things, the way they speak shows that they have not passed through the deeper work of grace. In this verse we can notice not only her lips slowly dropping sweet honey, but the things that are stored within her. "Honey and milk are under your tongue." The top of the tongue is where man takes in food, whereas under the tongue is where man stores food. This means that she has stored up these things; there are riches within her. She has more than enough food. Honey restores the weak ones, whereas milk feeds the immature ones. She has stored so many riches within her that food seems to be under her tongue and she can dispense to the needy ones at any time. However, she does not reveal all that she has. She is not like many people who exhibit on the outside all that they have inside. Honey and milk are under her tongue; they are not on her lips. (Watchman Nee, *The Song of Songs,* p. 72)

Further Reading: Life-study of Exodus, msg. 6; *Life-study of Song of Songs,* msg. 4; *The Song of Songs,* sec. 3

Enlightenment and inspiration: _____

_____

_____

_____

Morning Nourishment

Col. As therefore you have received the Christ, Jesus the
2:6-7 Lord, walk in Him, having been rooted and being
built up in Him...

11 In Him also you were circumcised with a circumcision not made with hands, in the putting off of
the body of the flesh, in the circumcision of Christ.

13 And you, though dead in your offenses and in the
uncircumcision of your flesh, He made alive together
with Him, having forgiven us all our offenses.

The section of Colossians which includes 2:8-15 is rather com-
plicated. It contains a number of important points. Many of these
points are related to Christ as the good land, as the rich soil in
which we have been rooted. The expression "having been rooted"
in verse 7 implies that there is soil....Having been rooted in the
soil, we grow with the elements we absorb from the soil. We know
that Christ as the soil is in our spirit. Now we must go on to see,
from verses 8 through 15, a description of the very soil in which
we have been rooted. These verses present a full description and
definition of the soil.

The first aspect of this very special soil is found in verse 9: "For
in Him dwells all the fullness of the Godhead bodily." We have
been rooted in the One in whom all the fullness of the Godhead
dwells bodily. We should not allow anyone to carry us away from
such a soil. To be carried away from this soil is to be uprooted from
it. When the book of Colossians was written, some were trying to
uproot the believers from Christ. The believers had been rooted in
Christ as the good land, as the One in whom all the fullness of the
Godhead dwells. Instead of allowing anyone to carry us away
from this soil, we must stay rooted in it. (*Life-study of Colossians,*
pp. 461-462)

Today's Reading

In Colossians 2:10 Paul continues, "And you have been made
full in Him, who is the Head of all rule and authority." Here we see
more concerning the substance of Christ as the soil. One aspect of

the soil is that of the fullness of the Godhead; another aspect is that Christ is the Head of all rule and authority. In Christ as the good land we have a number of different elements. The first element is all the fullness of the Godhead, and the second is the Head of all rule and authority.

In verses 11 through 15 we find more elements. Verse 11 [implies that]...the soil also includes the circumcision of Christ, which denotes cutting and killing. In the soil there is, therefore, a killing element. Verse 12, which says that we were buried together with Christ in baptism, indicates that the soil also contains the element of burial. In Christ as the soil there is a substance which causes us to be buried. After burial, we are raised up. In verse 12 Paul speaks of God who raised Christ from the dead. This expression indicates that in Christ as the soil there is an element which causes us to be raised up. According to verse 13, we also are made alive. There is an element in the soil which gives us life, enlivens us. In 1 Corinthians 15:45 Paul speaks of the life-giving Spirit. In Colossians 2:13 he uses the same Greek term for life-giving, only in the past tense. As the soil, Christ has made us alive; He has given us life.

In verses 14 and 15 Paul continues, "Wiping out the handwriting in ordinances, which was against us, which was contrary to us; and He has taken it out of the way, nailing it to the cross. Stripping off the rulers and the authorities, He made a display of them openly, triumphing over them in it." Here we have more elements that are found in Christ as the soil. The wiping out of the handwriting in ordinances is an element in the soil. The same is true of the stripping off of the rulers and the authorities, the making of a display of them openly, and the triumphing over them in the cross. As the soil, Christ includes all these marvelous elements. Praise Him that He is such a rich soil! We have been rooted in this soil. Day by day, our roots need to sink deeper into Christ as the unique soil. (*Life-study of Colossians,* pp. 462-463)

Further Reading: Life-study of Colossians, msg. 53

Enlightenment and inspiration: _____

_____

_____

Morning Nourishment

Col.
2:6-10

As therefore you have received the Christ, Jesus the Lord, walk in Him, having been rooted and being built up in Him, and being established in the faith even as you were taught, abounding in thanksgiving. Beware that no one carries you off as spoil through his philosophy and empty deceit, according to the tradition of men, according to the elements of the world, and not according to Christ; for in Him dwells all the fullness of the Godhead bodily, and you have been made full in Him, who is the Head of all rule and authority.

When we are rooted in Christ as the soil, the first thing to take place is that we are made full in Him (Col. 2:10). The phrase "made full" implies a great deal and requires an amplified translation in order to bring out its real significance. The Greek word implies completion, perfection, satisfaction, and full accomplishment. In Christ as the soil we are filled, completed, perfected, satisfied, and thoroughly supplied. We have pointed out that the first element of the soil is the fullness of the Godhead. As we absorb into our being the rich nourishment from the soil, we enjoy this fullness. Then this fullness makes us full, completes us, perfects us, satisfies us, accomplishes everything for us, and thoroughly supplies our every need. (*Life-study of Colossians,* pp. 463-464)

Today's Reading

This fullness is inexhaustible. Such an inexhaustible fullness is the first element of the rich soil in which we are rooted. God has planted us into a rich land. The first aspect of this land is the fullness of the Godhead, the expression of God in the old creation and in the new creation. Thus, the fullness implies the expression of God in the old creation and in the new creation. Having been planted into such rich soil, we absorb nourishment from the soil. The first element of the riches of the soil is the fullness. In this fullness we have been made full. Thus, we are short of nothing.

Paul wanted the Colossian believers to realize that since they

had been made full in Christ, they had no need to worship angels. Christ was the Head of all rule and authority, and angels
were just one item of God's creation. In the fullness we are made
full, complete, and perfect. Everything necessary is accomplished, and we are supplied and satisfied. Oh, this fullness is
all-inclusive. It includes righteousness, justification, holiness,
sanctification, and whatever we may need. Having been planted
into this fullness, we should simply absorb nourishment from it.
As we do so, we shall find that we have no lack. The experiences
of crucifixion and resurrection are in the fullness. Praise the
Lord that we may enjoy the universal, eternal, extensive, all-
inclusive fullness! This fullness dwells in Christ bodily. Since
Christ is the good land in which we have been rooted, we have
been rooted in this fullness; in it we have been made full, complete, and perfect. We have no need whatever.

Before we were rooted in Christ as the good land, we did not
have anything positive. Instead, we were involved with the
flesh, the ordinances, and the power of darkness. But now that
we have been rooted in the good land, the fullness has become
ours, and we are supplied with every positive thing. In this all-
inclusive and extensive fullness, we have everything. We have
God, we have an uplifted humanity, and we have divine attributes and human virtues. Do you need life? It is found in this fullness. Do you need love or patience? They also are included in the
fullness. Because this fullness is all-inclusive, it accomplishes
everything for us, it fully satisfies and supplies us, and it makes
us full, perfect, and complete. How rich is the soil in which we
have been rooted! It supplies us with everything, and we have no
lack. We have the all-inclusive, inexhaustible fullness. In this
universe there is such a thing that Paul in Colossians calls the
fullness. This fullness dwells in Christ bodily. In Him, the embodiment of the fullness of the Godhead, we are made full.
(*Life-study of Colossians,* pp. 464-465)

Further Reading: Life-study of Colossians, msg. 53

Enlightenment and inspiration: _____

_____

_____

_____

Morning Nourishment

Col. **Persevere in prayer, watching in it with thanks-**
4:2 **giving.**

Matt. **And after He sent the crowds away, He went up to**
14:23 **the mountain privately to pray. And when night**
fell, He was there alone.

6:6 **But you, when you pray, enter into your private**
room, and shut your door and pray to your Father
who is in secret; and your Father who sees in secret
will repay you.

If we would absorb the riches of Christ as the soil, we need to
have tender, new roots. Do not let yourself get old, but be fresh and
renewed day by day. Pray to the Lord, "Lord, I want my consecra-
tion to be fresh, and I want to open to You anew. I want my roots to
be tender that I may absorb Your riches. Lord, don't let my roots
get old." If our roots are tender and new to absorb the riches of
Christ, we shall grow automatically with the riches we assimilate. This is to enjoy Christ and to experience Him subjectively
daily and hourly. This will keep us from being defrauded of our
prize. But if we do not remain rooted in Him to absorb His riches,
in a subtle way the enemy will defraud us of the practical and con-
tinual enjoyment of Christ. (*Life-study of Colossians*, p. 487)

Today's Reading

We have heard a number of messages concerning who the
Lord is, what He is, and where He is. We have also learned how to
exercise our spirit to contact Him. But now we must take suffi-
cient time to absorb Him. We should not be lazy or indolent in this
matter....I can testify strongly that when we take time to enjoy
the Lord, all the elements of the rich soil are absorbed into us.

If we wish to be victorious, we must take time to absorb the
Lord. As we absorb Him into us for our enjoyment, we shall have
the fullness, the circumcision, the burial, the raising up, the im-
partation of life, the wiping out of the ordinances, and the stripping off of the power of darkness. Day by day we may enjoy the
rich Christ by absorbing Him into us.

If you see that we have been rooted in Christ as the rich soil, you will be comforted and encouraged. Do not be troubled by your weaknesses. Consider the rich soil in which you are rooted. In this soil do you not have the fullness, the circumcision, the burial, the raising up, the giving of life, the wiping out of the ordinances, and the stripping off of the powers of darkness? Forget your situation, your condition, your failures, and your weaknesses and simply take time to enjoy the Lord. Take time to absorb Him, to assimilate the rich elements from Him as the soil. If you take time to absorb the Lord, you will be able to testify that in Christ you have no lack.

Every morning we need to take an adequate amount of time to absorb the Lord. Although even ten minutes is good, it is best to spend thirty minutes to enjoy Him at the start of each new day. If you spend thirty minutes to absorb the Lord and to enjoy Him in the morning, you will not be bothered by negative things during the day....However, we should spend time with the Lord not only in the morning but also throughout the day. If we have a good time with the Lord in the morning, afternoon, and evening,...we shall also enjoy a feast. However, if we are not faithful to take time to absorb the Lord, our condition will gradually deteriorate. Our experience confirms this. Let us turn from our thought, emotion, and intention and open ourselves to the Lord, exercising our spirit to say, "O Lord Jesus, I love You, I worship You, and I adore You. Lord, I give myself to You. I give You my heart and everything concerning this day." As you contact the Lord in this way, do not be hurried. Take time, the more the better. As you spend time contacting the Lord, spontaneously you will absorb into you the riches of the soil. The fullness, the circumcision, the burial, the raising up, the imparting of life, the wiping out of the ordinances, and the stripping off of the authorities will be yours. All these facts in the book of Colossians will become your experience. (*Life-study of Colossians,* pp. 467-469)

Further Reading: Life-study of Colossians, msgs. 44, 46-48, 51-53, 55

Enlightenment and inspiration: _____

_____

_____

_____

Hymns, #196

1 Lord, the ancient types and symbols
    As our all Thyself portrayed;
  As was shadowed in those figures,
    Real to us Thou now art made.
  Contemplating such a picture,
    As we on its wonders gaze,
  How we marvel at Thy riches
    And our song of worship raise.

2 Lord, Thou art our true Passover,
    God passed over us thru Thee;
  By Thyself and Thy redemption
    We with God have harmony.
  Thou, the Lamb of God, redeemedst us
    With Thyself and with Thy blood;
  We apply Thy blood, our ransom,
    Eating Thee, our real food.

3 Lord, Thou art the Bread from heaven,
    The unleavened Bread of life;
  Eating Thee, with Thee we mingle,
    Ceasing from our sin and strife.
  Lamb and Bread are both Thy figures,
    Showing Thou art life to us;
  Feasting on Thee at Thy table,
    We enjoy Thy riches thus.

4 Lord, Thou art the Heav'nly Manna,
    As our daily food supply;
  Strengthening and energizing,
    All our need to satisfy.
  Living Rock Thou also art, Lord,
    Cleft for us with life to flow;
  Drinking of this living water,
    Thirst is quenched, Thy life we know.

5 Lord, Thou art the Land of Canaan—
    Elevated, rich and good,
  Flowing with both milk and honey
    In a glorious plenitude.
  By Thy surplus God we worship,
    In Thy fellowship we move;
  Thus in love we're joined together
    And God's building we will prove.

Composition for prophecy with main point and sub-points: _____

_____

_____

_____

_____

_____

_____

_____

_____

_____

_____

_____

_____

_____

_____

_____

_____

_____

_____

_____

_____

_____

_____

_____

_____

_____

_____

_____

_____

_____

_____

_____

_____

The Kingdom of the Son of the Father's Love

Scripture Reading: Col. 1:13; Acts 26:18; John 3:3, 5; Luke 17:20-21; Mark 9:1-2

Day 1
I. **The kingdom of God is the ruling, the reigning, of God with all its blessing and enjoyment (Mark 1:15):**
   A. The kingdom of God is God's reign in a general way from eternity past to eternity future and also God's reign in a particular way in the sense of life (Heb. 1:8; Psa. 145:13; Dan. 4:3; John 3:3, 5, 15).
   B. The kingdom of God is God Himself, and God Himself is life and everything as the content of the kingdom of God (Mark 1:15; cf. Eph. 4:18).
   C. The kingdom of God is the Savior, the Lord Jesus, as the seed of life sown into His believers and developing into a realm over which God can rule as His kingdom in His divine life (Luke 17:20-21; Mark 4:3, 26):
      1. The entrance into the kingdom is regeneration, and the development of the kingdom is the believers' growth in the divine life (John 3:5; 2 Pet. 1:3-11).
      2. The kingdom is the church life today, in which the faithful believers live (Rom. 14:17).
      3. The kingdom of God will develop into the coming kingdom as a reward to be inherited by the overcoming saints in the millennium (Gal. 5:21; Eph. 5:5; Rev. 20:4, 6).
      4. The kingdom will consummate in the New Jerusalem as the eternal realm of the eternal blessing of God's eternal life, which His redeemed will enjoy in the new heaven and new earth for eternity (21:1-4; 22:1-5, 14).
   D. The kingdom is the shining of the reality of the Lord Jesus; to be under His shining is to be in the kingdom (Mark 9:1-2).

Day 2 E. The kingdom of God as the reign of God is a
realm not only of the divine dominion but also of
the divine species, in which are all the divine
things (John 3:3, 5):
1. In John 3 the kingdom of God refers more to
the species of God than to the reign of God.
2. God became man to enter into the human
species, and man becomes God in life and
nature but not in the Godhead to enter into
the divine species (1:12-14; Rom. 8:3; 1:3-4).
3. To enter into the divine realm, the realm of
the divine species, we need to be born of God
to have the divine life and nature (John
1:12-13):
   a. We were regenerated of God to be the
   species of God and enter into the kingdom of God (3:3, 5).
   b. Our second birth caused us to enter into
   the kingdom of God to become the species
   of God; now we are God-men in the divine
   species, that is, in the kingdom of God.

Day 3 II. **The Father delivered us out of the authority
of darkness and transferred us into the
kingdom of the Son of His love (Col. 1:13):**
A. The authority of darkness denotes the authority
of Satan (Acts 26:18):
1. Darkness is Satan as death; thus, to be delivered out of the authority of darkness is to be
delivered from the devil, who has the might
of death (Heb. 2:14; John 17:15).
2. We have been delivered from the devil, Satan,
by the death of Christ and by the life of
Christ in resurrection (Col. 1:13; 2:14-15;
John 5:24).

Day 4 3. In Colossians the authority of darkness refers to the good aspects of culture and of our
character, disposition, and natural being.
4. Whenever we are in the natural man or live
in the self, we are under the control of the

authority of darkness; the only thing we can do is go to the cross and allow the cross to deal with every aspect of the satanic authority of darkness (Matt. 16:24; Col. 3:5-9).

Day 5

B. The kingdom of the Son is the authority of Christ (Rev. 11:15; 12:10):

1. The Son of God is the embodiment and expression of the divine life; hence, the kingdom of the Son is a realm of life (1 John 5:11-12; John 1:4).

2. The kingdom into which we have been transferred is the kingdom of the Son of God's love; this realm of life is in love, not in fear (Col. 1:13).

3. The kingdom in which we find ourselves today is a realm full of life, light, and love (1 Pet. 2:9).

4. The Son of the Father is the expression of the Father as the source of life (John 1:18, 4; 1 John 1:2):

   a. The Son of the Father's love is the object of the Father's love to be the embodiment of life to us in the divine love with the authority in resurrection (Matt. 3:17).

   b. The Son, as the embodiment of the divine life, is the object of the Father's love (17:5):

      1) The divine life embodied in the Son is given to us in the divine love.

      2) The object of the divine love becomes to us the embodiment of life in the divine love with the authority in resurrection; this is the kingdom of the Son of the Father's love.

Day 6

5. To be transferred into the kingdom of the Son of the Father's love is to be transferred into the Son, who is life to us (1 John 5:12):

   a. The Son in resurrection is now the life-giving Spirit, and He rules us in His

resurrection life with love (1 Pet. 1:3;
Rom. 6:4-5; 1 Cor. 15:45b).

b. When we live by the Son as our life in resurrection, we are living in His kingdom,
enjoying Him in the Father's love; here
we have the church life (Col. 3:4; John
6:57).

6. Although the kingdom of the Son of the
Father's love comprises the present age,
the coming age, and the eternal age, the
emphasis in Colossians 1:13 is on the kingdom of the Son of the Father's love in this
age, the age of the church:

a. Because the Father delights in His Son,
the kingdom of the Son of the Father's
love is a pleasant thing, a matter of delight (Matt. 3:17; 17:5).

b. The church life today is the kingdom of
the Son of the Father's love, which is as
delightful to God the Father as the Son of
God is.

c. God the Father loves the delightful part
of the kingdom just as much as He loves
His delightful Son.

Morning Nourishment

Mark ...The kingdom of God has drawn near. Repent and
1:15 believe in the gospel.
4:26 And He said, So is the kingdom of God: as if a man cast
        seed on the earth.
Luke And when He was questioned by the Pharisees *as to*
17:20-21 when the kingdom of God was coming, He answered
        them and said, The kingdom of God does not come
        with observation....For behold, the kingdom of God is
        in the midst of you.
Rom. For the kingdom of God is not eating and drinking, but
14:17 righteousness and peace and joy in the Holy Spirit.

The kingdom of God is the Savior (Luke 17:21) as the seed of
life, sown into His believers, God's chosen people (Mark 4:3, 26),
and developing into a realm which God may rule as His kingdom
in His divine life. Its entrance is regeneration (John 3:5), and its
development is the believers' growth in the divine life (2 Pet.
1:3-11). It is the church life today, in which the faithful believers
live (Rom. 14:17), and it will develop into the coming kingdom as
an inheritance reward (Gal. 5:21; Eph. 5:5) to the overcoming
saints in the millennium (Rev. 20:4, 6). Eventually, it will consummate in the New Jerusalem as the eternal kingdom of God, an
eternal realm of the eternal blessing of God's eternal life for all
God's redeemed to enjoy in the new heaven and new earth for
eternity (Rev. 21:1-4; 22:1-5, 14). Such a kingdom, the kingdom of
God, is what the Savior preached in Luke 4 as the gospel, the good
news. (*Life-study of Luke,* p. 95)

Today's Reading

What is "the kingdom of God"? We must understand that the
kingdom of God is God Himself....In the animal world are animals,
and in the vegetable world are vegetables. Likewise, in the human
world, the human kingdom, are human beings. The human world
ceases to exist when human beings are removed from it. In the
same principle, the kingdom of God is God Himself, and it is God
Himself who becomes everything as the content of the kingdom of

God. If God leaves, the kingdom of God will have nothing left in it.

In order for a dog or a cow to enter and participate in the human world, the human kingdom, it has to receive the human life by being born again. A dog or a cow can be in the human kingdom only by birth. I was born a man with man's life, so naturally I entered into the human world, the human kingdom....If we want to obtain the citizenship of a certain country or join a certain club in society, we need to meet certain requirements or pay a fee. To be in the human kingdom, however, the only requirement is to be born.

Now we all understand that the kingdom of God is God Himself. Following John the Baptist, the Lord Jesus also said, "The kingdom of God has drawn near" (Mark 1:15)....To proclaim that the kingdom of God has drawn near is to declare that God Himself has drawn near and that men should get ready to receive Him into them. The way to prepare is to put away the old, natural concepts and to hold on to the New Testament revelation, knowing that to enter into God's kingdom is to receive God Himself. This is the central thought of the preaching of John the Baptist as the forerunner in the New Testament dispensation.

We must have a clear understanding of the kingdom of God. God's kingdom is God Himself, and God's kingdom has God as its content. Moreover, this content is Jesus Christ, who is God incarnated to be a man and who is God Himself as the reality of the kingdom of God. John 3:3 says, "Unless one is born anew, he cannot see the kingdom of God." God's kingdom is a divine realm, and man must have the life of God to enter into it. As we said before, life itself is a kingdom, a world, and a regulating element. Similarly, God's kingdom is God Himself, and God Himself is life, having the nature, ability, and shape of the divine life, which forms the realm of God's reigning. (*The Economy of God and the Mystery of the Transmission of the Divine Trinity,* pp. 39-40, 43-45)

Further Reading: Life-study of Luke, msgs. 11, 22; *The Economy of God and the Mystery of the Transmission of the Divine Trinity,* ch. 3; *The Conclusion of the New Testament,* msg. 240

Enlightenment and inspiration: _____

_____

_____

_____

Morning Nourishment

John But as many as received Him, to them He gave the
1:12-14 authority to become children of God, to those who
believe into His name, who were begotten not of
blood, nor of the will of the flesh, nor of the will of
man, but of God. And the Word became flesh and
tabernacled among us (and we beheld His glory,
glory as of the only Begotten from the Father), full
of grace and reality.

  3:3 ...Unless one is born anew, he cannot see the kingdom of God.

  5 ...Unless one is born of water and the Spirit, he cannot enter into the kingdom of God.

We are regenerated of God the Spirit to be spirits—gods
(John 3:6b) belonging to the species of God to see and enter into
the kingdom of God (vv. 3, 5). John 1 tells us how we received the
authority to be the children of God. Then John 3 speaks of regeneration again. Verse 6 says, "That which is born of the flesh is
flesh, and that which is born of the Spirit is spirit." We are the
flesh and born of the flesh in our natural life. But...we [also] are
born of the Spirit, and the Spirit is God. John 4:24 tells us clearly
that God is Spirit. Because we are born of God the Spirit, we
must be gods in life and in nature but not in the Godhead.

We must not forget that we are God-men belonging to God's
species. As God-men born of God and belonging to God's species,
we cannot speak to our spouse in a loose way. A husband must be
a God-man, living as a God-man. To be merely a good man is far
away from God's good pleasure. We need to see that we are
God-men, born of God and belonging to God's species. This is the
beginning of the God-man living. (*The God-man Living*, pp. 8-9)

Today's Reading

The kingdom of God is the reign of God. This divine reign is a
realm, not only of the divine dominion but also of the divine species, in which are all the divine things. The vegetable kingdom is
a realm of the vegetable species, and the animal kingdom is a

realm of the animal species. In the same way, the kingdom of God is a realm of the divine species.

God became flesh to enter into the human species, and man becomes God in His life and nature, but not in His divine Godhead, to enter into His divine species. In John 3 the kingdom of God refers more to the species of God than to the reign of God.... To enter into the divine realm, the realm of the divine species, we need to be born of God to have the divine nature and life.

That man was created in the image of God and after His likeness indicates that man was created in God's kind, in God's species. Genesis 1 says that each of the living things was created after its kind. But God created man, not after man's kind, but in God's image and after God's likeness to be God's kind.

The believers, who are born of God by regeneration to be His children in His life and nature, but not in His Godhead (John 1:12-13), are more in God's kind than Adam was. Adam had only the outward appearance of God without the inward reality, the divine life. We have the reality of the divine life within us and we are being transformed and conformed to the Lord's image in our entire being. It is logical to say that all the children of God are in the divine realm of the divine species.

If the children of God are not in God's kind, in God's species, in what kind are they? If they are not gods, what are they? We all who are born of God are gods. But for utterance, due to the theological misunderstanding, it is better to say that we are God-men in the divine species, that is, in the kingdom of God.

These God-men, who are children born of God, not only constitute the house of God (1 Tim. 3:15; 1 Pet. 4:17; John 14:2) but also are the constituents with which the Body of Christ is built up, and the Body of Christ will consummate the New Jerusalem as the eternal kingdom of God and of Christ (1 Cor. 6:9; Eph. 5:5; 2 Pet. 1:11; Rev. 11:15). (*Crystallization-study of the Gospel of John*, pp. 123-124)

Further Reading: The God-man Living, msg. 1; *Crystallization-study of the Gospel of John,* msg. 12

Enlightenment and inspiration: _____

_____

_____

_____

Morning Nourishment

Col. Who delivered us out of the authority of darkness
1:13 and transferred *us* into the kingdom of the Son of
His love.

Acts To open their eyes, to turn *them* from darkness to
26:18 light and *from* the authority of Satan to God, that
they may receive forgiveness of sins and an inheritance among those who have been sanctified by
faith in Me.

Heb. Since therefore the children have shared in blood
2:14 and flesh, He also Himself in like manner partook
of the same, that through death He might destroy
him who has the might of death, that is, the devil.

John I do not ask that You would take them out of the
17:15 world, but that You would keep them out of *the
hands of* the evil *one*.

In Colossians 1:13 Paul says, "Who delivered us out of the
authority of darkness and transferred us into the kingdom of
the Son of His love." Paul's word here corresponds to the word
given him by the Lord on the way to Damascus. According to
Acts 26:18, the Lord charged Paul, "To open their eyes, to turn
them from darkness to light and from the authority of Satan
to God, that they may receive forgiveness of sins and an inheritance among those who have been sanctified by faith in Me."
Both in this verse and in Colossians 1:12 and 13 Paul speaks
of darkness, light, authority, those who are sanctified, and
the portion or the inheritance. No doubt, Paul's word to the
Colossians reflects the Lord's word to him at the time of his
conversion. (*Life-study of Colossians,* p. 27)

Today's Reading

The authority of darkness denotes the authority of Satan.
God is light, and Satan is darkness. Satan's authority of darkness is the authority of evil in the heavenlies, in the air (Eph.

6:12). This evil refers to something that is in rebellion against God. The authority of evil, of rebellion, in the heavenlies is the kingdom of Satan, the authority of darkness (Matt. 12:26).

Darkness is related to death. Where darkness is, there death is also. This darkness is opposed to light, which is related to life. Satan, darkness, and death stand in opposition to God, light, and life. According to 1 Peter 2:9, we have been called out of darkness into God's marvelous light. Darkness is Satan as death, but light is God Himself as life.

To be delivered out of the authority of darkness is to be delivered from the devil, who has the might of death (Heb. 2:14; John 17:15). We have been delivered from the devil, Satan, by the death of Christ (Col. 2:15) and by the life of Christ in resurrection (John 5:24).

We have seen that the authority of darkness is the kingdom of Satan and that Satan himself is darkness. The kingdom of Satan is a system. Not everything in this system is evil. On the contrary, many things are good, or at least are considered good by society. Satan uses various things, both good and evil, to systematize people and to keep them in his system. For those who are fond of gambling, Satan uses gambling to systematize them. Therefore, in his kingdom there is a ministry, a department, of gambling. However, Satan realizes that others may appreciate knowledge. In order to systematize them, Satan has a department of knowledge in his kingdom. Most people condemn gambling, but hardly anyone condemns knowledge. If we encourage others to stay away from the evil aspects of Satan's system, we shall be appreciated. Satan systematizes some people by luring them into practicing evil, but he systematizes others through their efforts to suppress evil. (*Life-study of Colossians,* pp. 28-29)

Further Reading: Life-study of Colossians, msgs. 3-4; *The Conclusion of the New Testament,* msgs. 240, 244; *Life-study of Acts,* msg. 69

Enlightenment and inspiration: _____

_____

_____

_____

Morning Nourishment

Matt. Then Jesus said to His disciples, If anyone wants
16:24 to come after Me, let him deny himself and take up
his cross and follow Me.

Col. Put to death therefore your members which are on
3:5 the earth: fornication, uncleanness, passion, evil
desire, and greediness, which is idolatry.

8 But now, you also, put away all *these* things: wrath,
anger, malice, blasphemy, foul abusive language
out of your mouth.

In our daily lives, many of us are still under some aspect of the
satanic authority of darkness. Unconsciously, subconsciously, and
spontaneously we live according to the self, not according to
Christ. How much of each day do you live in the spirit and walk
according to the spirit? How much time do you still live and walk
in the self? Whenever we live in the self, we are under the control
of the authority of darkness and are systematized by Satan. We
are under Satan's control whenever we are in the natural man or
live according to the self. Because of this satanic control, many
have the sense that they are in darkness, that they have no light.
The reason they are under darkness is that they are still controlled in some way by the authority of darkness. All of mankind,
religious and nonreligious ones alike, are in darkness. In this
darkness Satan's authority is exercised in various ways to systematize people and to control them. (*Life-study of Colossians,* p. 31)

Today's Reading

If we would have the proper understanding of Colossians 1:13,
we need to consider this verse in the context of the whole Epistle.
Considering the book as a whole, we see that the authority of
darkness includes the Jewish religion with its observances, especially circumcision; it also includes Gentile ordinances, philosophy, mysticism, and asceticism. Throughout the world today
people are under darkness, just as they were when the book of
Colossians was written. To be in darkness is simply to be without
light. Every university and every social group is under the

authority of darkness. Every aspect of society, including Christianity, is in darkness. Do not think that darkness is found only where there is evil. Paul was telling the Colossians that God had delivered them out from under the authority of darkness, that is, out from legalities, ordinances, practices, asceticism, mysticism, and philosophy. Although these include the highest products of culture, they are nonetheless the authority of darkness by which Satan controls people.

Satan has many ways to control Christians. New ones who visit our meetings may be under the authority of darkness, especially the darkness of doctrine and of doctrinal understanding. Most Christians are under some form of doctrinal control. They are not aware that this control is the authority of darkness.

Others are under the authority of darkness because they live according to some natural virtue. They may be kind or humble in a natural way. However, even through virtues such as these, Satan may control us and hold us under the authority of darkness. Some do not receive light because they are under the darkness of their natural virtue. Every natural virtue is an aspect of the authority of darkness.

Many saints are controlled by their disposition, either by a quick disposition or by a slow one. Whatever our disposition may be, Satan can use it to control us.

When you read this word...about all the ways Satan uses to keep us in darkness and to control us, you may wonder how we should live. It may seem that we have no way to go on. Whatever we are, whatever we do, whatever we think, and whatever we say—all is under the authority of darkness. This is our actual situation. The only thing we can do is go to the cross and allow the cross to deal with every aspect of the satanic authority of darkness. The cross is our unique way. We also must believe Paul's word in 1:13. We have already been delivered out of the authority of darkness. (*Life-study of Colossians,* pp. 30-32)

Further Reading: Life-study of Colossians, msgs. 4-5

Enlightenment and inspiration: _____

_____

_____

_____

Morning Nourishment

1 John   And this is the testimony, that God gave to us eternal
5:11   life and this life is in His Son.

1 Pet.   But you are a chosen race, a royal priesthood, a holy
2:9   nation, a people acquired for a possession, so that
         you may tell out the virtues of Him who has called
         you out of darkness into His marvelous light.

John   No one has ever seen God; the only begotten Son, who
1:18   is in the bosom of the Father, He has declared *Him*.

Matt.   ...This is My Son, the Beloved, in whom I have found
3:17   My delight.

We have been not only delivered out of the authority of darkness, but also transferred into the kingdom of the Son of God's love. The kingdom of the Son is the authority of Christ (Rev. 11:15; 12:10)....The Son of the Father is the expression of the Father as the source of life (John 1:18, 4; 1 John 1:2). The Father as the source of life is expressed in the Son.

The Son of the Father's love is the object of the Father's love to be the embodiment of life to us in the divine love with the authority in resurrection. The Son, as the embodiment of the divine life, is the object of the Father's love. The divine life embodied in the Son is given to us in the divine love. Therefore, the object of the divine love becomes to us the embodiment of life in the divine love with the authority in resurrection. This is the kingdom of the Son of His love. (*Life-study of Colossians,* p. 32)

Today's Reading

It is easier to give an illustration of the kingdom of the Son of His love than it is to give an adequate definition of it. Consider your experience. Coming to realize that the Lord Jesus is so loving and lovable, we began to love Him. As we love the Lord Jesus, we are conscious of a sweet sense of love. Not only does this sense of love include the Lord Jesus, but it also includes us. We realize that we also are the objects of the divine love. As objects of this divine love, we spontaneously come under a certain control or ruling. Before we began to love the Lord Jesus, we were free to do whatever we wanted. But the more we say, "Lord Jesus, I love You," the less freedom we have. Before we began to love the Lord Jesus, we did not sense this ruling or restriction. We could mistreat people or engage in worldly entertainments without any sense of inward restriction. But as those who love the Lord Jesus, we have come under His rule. This rule is not harsh; on the contrary, it is sweet and pleasant. Oh, we are restricted and ruled in such a sweet way! Because of the pleasantness of the Lord's rule in us, we do not care even to speak a vain word or to have a thought that is displeasing to Him. We are ruled and restricted to the uttermost in the sweetness of love. This is the kingdom of the Son of His love.

The more we are willing to be restricted and ruled by the Lord Jesus out of our love for Him, the more we shall grow in life, even in the abundance of life. This indicates that the kingdom of the Son of His love is for our enjoyment of Christ as life. Here we are freed from everything other than Christ, not only from evil things, but also from things such as philosophy, ordinances, observances, and asceticism. When we were holding to our philosophy, ethics, asceticism, and ordinances, we were under the authority of darkness. But God has delivered us out of this authority and has transferred us into a kingdom of love that is full of life and light. Here we have no observances, rituals, ordinances, practices, philosophies, mysticism, Gnosticism, or asceticism. We just have Christ, the Son of His love. Here we have love, light, and life. This is to live by Christ.

To live by Christ means that we do not live by anything other than Christ. If we see what it is to live by Christ, we shall realize that many of us are still under some form of control established by the self, a control set up and carried out by the self....This causes us to be held under the authority of darkness. Because... [of this],we have little enjoyment of Christ as the portion of the saints. (*Life-study of Colossians,* pp. 32-34)

Further Reading: Life-study of Colossians, msgs. 4-5

Enlightenment and inspiration: _____

_____

_____

_____

Morning Nourishment

1 John He who has the Son has the life; he who does not
5:12 have the Son of God does not have the life.

Col. When Christ our life is manifested, then you also
3:4 will be manifested with Him in glory.

John As the living Father has sent Me and I live because
6:57 of the Father, so he who eats Me, he also shall live
because of Me.

Matt. ...This is My Son, the Beloved, in whom I have
3:17 found My delight.

To be transferred into the kingdom of the Son of the Father's
love is to be transferred into the Son who is life to us (1 John 5:12).
The Son in resurrection (1 Pet. 1:3; Rom. 6:4-5) is now the life-
giving Spirit (1 Cor. 15:45b). He rules us in His resurrection life
with love. This is the kingdom of the Son of the Father's love.
When we live by the Son as our life in resurrection, we are living
in His kingdom, enjoying Him in the Father's love.

We have been transferred into a realm where we are ruled in
love with life. Here, under the heavenly ruling and restriction, we
have genuine freedom, the proper freedom in love, with life, and
under light. This is what it means to be delivered out of the authority of darkness and transferred into the kingdom of the Son of
His love. Here in this kingdom we enjoy Christ and have the
church life. Here there is no opinion or division. Here we have one
thing: the church life with Christ as everything to us. This is the
revelation of the book of Colossians. (*Life-study of Colossians,* p. 35)

Today's Reading

In Colossians the authority of darkness refers to the good
aspects of culture and of our character, disposition, and natural
being. The authority of darkness includes our virtues, religion,
philosophy, observances, ordinances, principles, and ethical
standards. God has delivered us out of all this and has transferred us into the kingdom of the Son of His love, where we live
under a heavenly rule and restriction. In this kingdom we are
not under a harsh rule, but under the loving rule of the Son.

Here we do not sense that we are under righteousness, power, or authority, but under the loving and lovable Lord Jesus. The more we tell the Lord Jesus that we love Him, the more we are freed on the one hand, and the more we are restricted and ruled on the other hand. Because we love Him, we desire to take Him as our person and as our life. This is the proper Christian life for the church life. (*Life-study of Colossians,* pp. 35-36)

The kingdom of the Son of God's love comprises three ages: the present age, in which the church is; the coming age, in which the millennial kingdom will be; and the eternal age with the New Jerusalem in the new heaven and the new earth. These three aspects of the kingdom are considered by Paul in Colossians 1:13 as the kingdom of the Son of God's love.

The words "the Son of God" are a delight to the Father's ears. When the Lord Jesus was baptized, the Father declared, "This is My Son, the Beloved, in whom I have found My delight" (Matt. 3:17). When the Lord was transfigured, the Father made the same declaration (Matt. 17:5). Because the Father delights in His Son, the kingdom of the Son of the Father's love is a pleasant thing, a matter of delight.

The stress in Colossians 1:13 is the kingdom of the Son of God's love in this age, which is the reality of the church. The church life today is the kingdom of the Son of God's love which is as delightful to God the Father as the Son of God is. We, the believers, all have been transferred into this delightful kingdom of the Son of God's love. God the Father loves the delightful part of the kingdom just as He loves His delightful Son as His own. So, the church, as the delightful part of the divine kingdom, is considered a great blessing to God's redeemed people by the apostle Paul in the book of Colossians, a book which is on Christ as the all-inclusive portion of God's people (Col. 1:12). (*The Conclusion of the New Testament,* pp. 2583-2584)

Further Reading: Life-study of Colossians, msgs. 4-5; *The Conclusion of the New Testament,* msg. 244

Enlightenment and inspiration: _____

_____

_____

_____

Hymns, #941

1   God's kingdom is God's reigning,
     His glory to maintain;
   It is His sovereign ruling,
     His order to sustain.
   He exercises fully
     His own authority
   Within His kingdom ever
     And to eternity.

2   Upon the throne, the center
     Of government divine,
   God reigns, and with His purpose
     Brings everything in line.
   God's headship and His lordship
     He only can maintain
   As King within His kingdom,
     O'er everything to reign.

3   By reigning in His kingdom
     God worketh all His will,
   And under His dominion
     His purpose doth fulfill.
   'Tis only in God's kingdom
     His blessing we may know;
   'Tis from His throne almighty
     The stream of life doth flow.

4   Submitted to God's ruling,
     All virtue thus will win;
   Rebellion to His Headship
     Is but the root of sin.
   The evil aim of Satan—
     God's throne to overthrow;
   Our aim and goal is ever
     His rule to fully know.

5   Within God's sovereign kingdom
     His Christ is magnified;
   When Christ in life is reigning,
     The Father's glorified.
   When God is in dominion,
     All things are truly blessed;
   When Christ for God is reigning,
     God's glory is expressed.

6   In fulness of the seasons
     God's Christ will head up all,
Then all will own His reigning
     And worship, great and small.
Such reign in life and glory
     The Church e'en now foretastes,
And to His rule submitting
     Unto His kingdom hastes.

Composition for prophecy with main point and sub-points: _____

_____

_____

_____

_____

_____

_____

_____

_____

_____

_____

_____

_____

_____

_____

_____

_____

_____

_____

_____

_____

_____

_____

_____

_____

_____

_____

_____

_____

_____

_____

_____

The Stewardship of God
to Complete the Word of God and
to Present Every Man Full-grown in Christ

Scripture Reading: Col. 1:24—2:2

Day 1   **I. We need to follow the pattern of Paul to be a faithful minister of the church according to the stewardship of God (1 Tim. 1:16; Col. 1:24-25):**

A. The desire of God's heart is to dispense Himself into man; this is the central point of the whole Bible (Gen. 2:7-9; John 10:10b; Eph. 3:8-11).

B. Because our Father has a great family, a divine household, and such vast riches, there is the need in His household for many stewards to dispense these riches to His children; this dispensing is the stewardship (v. 2; 1 Cor. 9:17).

C. A steward is a household administrator, a dispenser, one who dispenses the household supply to its members; the apostles were appointed by the Lord to be such stewards, dispensing God's mysteries, which are Christ as the mystery of God and the church as the mystery of Christ, to the believers (Col. 2:2; Eph. 3:4; 1 Cor. 4:1).

D. In this dispensing ministry it is most important that stewards be found faithful; as faithful stewards, we need to learn not to care about being criticized by others and not to criticize or examine ourselves (vv. 1-5).

Day 2   **II. For the sake of His Body, which is the church, the faithful stewards of God fill up that which is lacking of the afflictions of Christ (Col. 1:24):**

A. The afflictions of Christ are of two categories: those for accomplishing redemption, which were completed by Christ Himself, and those for producing and building the church, which need to be filled up by the apostles and the believers (John

12:24-26; Luke 12:50; Mark 10:38-39; Phil. 3:10; Isa. 53:3-5; Rev. 1:9; 2 Tim. 2:10; 2 Cor. 1:5-6).

B. The fact that Paul mentions the afflictions of Christ in connection with the stewardship of God indicates that the stewardship can be carried out only through suffering (1 Pet. 4:1, 10; 2 Cor. 6:8; cf. Psa. 91:1-2; 31:20).

Day 3 III. **The faithful stewards of God labor and struggle to complete the word of God (Col. 1:25; Acts 20:26-27):**

A. In the New Testament the apostles, especially the apostle Paul, completed the word of God in the mystery of God, which is Christ, and in the mystery of Christ, which is the church, to give us a full revelation of God's economy (Eph. 5:32; Col. 2:2; Eph. 3:4).

B. The mystery concerning Christ and the church was hidden from eternity and from all the times until the New Testament age, when it is being manifested to the saints, including all of us, the believers in Christ (Col. 1:26).

C. We need to fulfill our responsibility to complete the word of God in the sense of fully preaching the word, declaring all the counsel of God; this means that as we contact people, we must progressively, continually, and gradually preach the word of God in full (Acts 20:26-27).

D. The goal of the Lord's recovery is the completion of the word of God:

1. If we would be those who complete the word of God, we must minister Christ as the life-giving Spirit and stand with the church as the living expression of Christ on the proper ground of locality; this is our burden, our ministry, and our warfare.

2. Without the completion of the word of God, God's purpose cannot be fulfilled, and Christ cannot obtain His bride or come with His kingdom.

Day 4   **IV. The goal of Paul's ministry was to present every man full-grown in Christ (Col. 1:28-29):**

A. Paul announced the indwelling Christ in all wisdom for every man's full growth in Christ (Acts 20:20, 31; Col. 2:2-3; cf. 2 Chron. 1:10).

B. Paul labored and struggled according to Christ's operation within him in power, the power of the resurrection life (Phil. 3:10; Eph. 1:19; 3:7, 20):

1. In order to present every man full-grown in Christ, we must minister Christ to them as the portion of the saints, the reality of the good land, the all-inclusive One who is the centrality and universality of God's economy (Col. 1:12, 15, 18-19, 27; 2:3, 9, 16-17; 3:4, 11).

2. In order to present every man full-grown in Christ, we must minister the unsearchable riches of Christ for the building up of the church to fulfill God's eternal purpose (Eph. 3:8-11).

Day 5   3. In order to present every man full-grown in Christ, we must complete the word of God with the full revelation of Christ and the church (Col. 1:25-28).

4. In order to present every man full-grown in Christ, we must minister Christ as the mystery of God, that is, as the embodiment of God (2:2, 9).

5. In order to present every man full-grown in Christ, we must minister the church as the mystery of Christ, the expression of Christ (Eph. 3:4; 1:23).

6. In order to present every man full-grown in Christ, we must minister Christ as life to His members so that they may live by Him and grow with Him unto maturity (Col. 3:4; John 6:57; 14:19; Gal. 2:20; Eph. 4:13, 15).

Day 6   7. In order to present every man full-grown in Christ, we must be concerned about the condition of their hearts (Col. 2:1-2):

   a. If the hearts of the Colossians were comforted and knit together in love, the result
would be all the riches of the full assurance of understanding concerning Christ
as the mystery of God.

   b. It is only after their hearts have been
comforted, cherished, that the saints can
receive the revelation concerning Christ;
we must look to the Lord for the grace
to comfort all the distracted, dissatisfied, and disappointed hearts (Eph. 5:29;
cf. Isa. 61:1-2).

   c. If we would have all the riches of the full
assurance of understanding concerning
Christ as the mystery of God, every part
of our being must be exercised (Col. 2:2;
1 Tim. 4:7b):

     1) Due to our lack of exercise, we may
not have the full assurance of understanding concerning the recovery, the
kind of assurance that martyrs have
when they lay down their lives for the
Lord (Acts 1:8).

     2) When our entire being is exercised to
love the Lord Jesus, we shall gain the
full knowledge of Him (Mark 12:30;
Deut. 6:5).

Morning Nourishment

Col. 1:25	**Of which I became a minister according to the stewardship of God, which was given to me for you...**
Eph. 3:2	**If indeed you have heard of the stewardship of the grace of God which was given to me for you.**
8-9	**To me, less than the least of all saints, was this grace given to announce to the Gentiles the unsearchable riches of Christ as the gospel and to enlighten all** *that they may see* **what the economy of the mystery is, which throughout the ages has been hidden in God, who created all things.**
1 Cor. 9:17	**If I do this of my own will, I have a reward; but if not of my own will, I am entrusted with a stewardship.**

For the sake of the full expression of God, there is the need for the stewardship of God [Col. 1:25]....At the time of Paul, many rich families had stewards whose responsibility was to distribute food and other supplies to members of the household. Our Father has a great family, a divine household. Because our Father has such vast riches, there is the need in His household for many stewards to dispense these riches to His children. This dispensing is the stewardship,...and this stewardship is the ministry in the New Testament. The New Testament ministry is the dispensing of the unsearchable riches of the all-inclusive Christ into the members of God's family. The apostle Paul dispensed the riches of Christ into the saints. This is what we are doing in the ministry today. (*Life-study of Colossians,* pp. 89-90)

Today's Reading

The stewardship of God is according to the economy of God. With God it is a matter of economy; with us it is a matter of stewardship. All the saints, no matter how insignificant they may seem to be, have a ministry according to God's economy. This means that every saint can dispense the riches of Christ into others.

The desire of God's heart is to dispense Himself into man. This is the central point of the whole Bible. God's economy is to carry out the dispensing of Himself into man. We share in this economy through our stewardship, our ministry of dispensing the riches of Christ. After the riches of Christ have been dispensed into us, we need to take up the burden to dispense them into others. With God these riches are His economy; with us they are the stewardship; and when they are dispensed by us into others, they become God's dispensing. When God's economy reaches us, it becomes our stewardship. When we carry out our stewardship by dispensing Christ into others, it becomes the dispensing of God into them. Hence, we have the economy, the stewardship, and the dispensing.

Those who bear responsibility in the local churches need to share in the stewardship of God. This means that the elders should be those who take the lead to dispense the riches of Christ into others. Although Christ is all-inclusive and preeminent, there is still the need for Him to be dispensed into the members of God's family. This dispensing takes place through the stewardship. Hence, between the unsearchably rich Christ and the members of His Body, there is the need of the stewardship. All those who take the lead in the Lord's recovery and have responsibility for the care of the churches need to realize that they have a part in such a divine stewardship. We are not here to carry on an ordinary Christian work. For instance, we are not concerned merely with teaching the Bible in an outward way. Rather, we desire to serve the riches of Christ to all the members of God's family. In our conversation with one another, we need to minister the riches of Christ. Even when we are invited to the homes of the saints for dinner, we need to dispense the riches of Christ. This is the stewardship of God.

Every member of the Body of Christ has a part in this stewardship. In Ephesians 3:8 Paul refers to himself as "less than the least of all saints." This indicates that Paul was even smaller than we are. If Paul could be a steward, then we also can be stewards and dispense the riches of Christ into others. (*Life-study of Colossians,* pp. 90-91)

Further Reading: Life-study of Colossians, msg. 11; *Life-study of 1 Corinthians,* msg. 34

Enlightenment and inspiration: _____

_____

_____

_____

Morning Nourishment

Col.   I now rejoice in my sufferings on your behalf and fill
1:24   up on my part that which is lacking of the afflictions of
       Christ in my flesh for His Body, which is the church.

John   Truly, truly, I say to you, Unless the grain of wheat
12:24 falls into the ground and dies, it abides alone; but if it
       dies, it bears much fruit.

26   If anyone serves Me, let him follow Me; and where I
       am, there also My servant will be. If anyone serves
       Me, the Father will honor him.

Phil. To know Him and the power of His resurrection and
3:10   the fellowship of His sufferings, being conformed to
       His death.

2 Tim. Therefore I endure all things for the sake of the cho-
2:10   sen ones, that they themselves also may obtain the
       salvation which is in Christ Jesus with eternal glory.

The afflictions of Christ are of two categories: those for accomplishing redemption, which have been completed by Christ
Himself; and those for producing and building the church, which
need to be filled up by the apostles and the believers [Col. 1:24].

The fact that Paul mentions the afflictions of Christ in connection with the stewardship of God indicates that the stewardship can be carried out only through suffering. If we desire to
share in the stewardship of God, we must be prepared to suffer.
All those who participate in the service of the church or in the
ministry must be ready to partake of the afflictions of a steward.
This means that we must be willing to pay whatever price is necessary to fulfill our stewardship. (*Life-study of Colossians*, p. 92)

Today's Reading

When we give or receive hospitality, we need to carry out our
stewardship by dispensing the riches of Christ into others. However, to provide hospitality may involve a kind of suffering. In
like manner, to be the guest in someone's home also may be a
cause of suffering. I have been a guest in the homes of many
saints. The hosts have invariably taken care of me in a

marvelous way, doing everything necessary to meet my needs. Nevertheless, I suffered simply because I was not in my own home....However, I am happy to testify that many have spoken of the nourishment, edification, and strengthening they have received through sharing in hospitality, as either a host or a guest. This indicates that to carry out the stewardship of God by dispensing the riches of Christ into the members of God's royal family is worth any kind of suffering, great or small.

Christ, of course, took the lead to suffer for the producing and building up of His Body. But the apostles and believers must follow Christ's footsteps in suffering this kind of affliction....[John 12:24] does not speak of Christ's redeeming death, but of His producing, generating death. Christ fell into the ground and died as a grain of wheat in order to produce many grains for the church. According to John 12:26, those who desire to serve Him must follow Him in this regard.

In Philippians 3:10 Paul speaks of knowing the fellowship of Christ's sufferings. These sufferings are not for redemption, but for the building up of the Body. We cannot have fellowship in Christ's sufferings for redemption, but we need to have much fellowship in Christ's sufferings for the church.

In 2 Timothy 2:10 Paul says, "Therefore I endure all things for the sake of the chosen ones." This verse is a further indication that Paul suffered for the sake of the chosen ones, God's chosen people.

Furthermore, 2 Corinthians 1:5 and 6 say, "For even as the sufferings of the Christ abound unto us, so through the Christ our comfort also abounds. But whether we are afflicted, it is for your comforting and salvation; or whether we are comforted, it is for your comforting, which operates in the endurance of the same sufferings which we also suffer." This is another indication of how much Paul suffered for the saints. (*Life-study of Colossians,* pp. 93, 98-101)

Further Reading: Life-study of Colossians, msgs. 11-12

Enlightenment and inspiration: _____

_____

_____

_____

Morning Nourishment

Col. **Of which I became a minister according to the**
1:25 **stewardship of God, which was given to me for**
you, to complete the word of God.

Acts **Therefore I testify to you on this day that I am**
20:26-27 **clean from the blood of all men, for I did not shrink**
from declaring to you all the counsel of God.

Eph. **This mystery is great, but I speak with regard to**
5:32 **Christ and the church.**

The completion of the word of God includes the great mystery of Christ and the church (Eph. 5:32); the full revelation concerning Christ, the Head (Col. 1:26-27; 2:19; 3:11); and the full revelation concerning the church, the Body (Eph. 3:3-6). Not only should these matters be impressed upon us; they should be infused into our being. May the Lord make us all clear concerning His recovery and concerning the wrestling for the completion of the word of God. If we would be those who complete the word of God, we must minister Christ as the life-giving Spirit and stand with the church as the living expression of Christ on the proper ground of locality. This is our burden, our ministry, and our warfare. (*Life-study of Colossians,* p. 112)

Today's Reading

Although the divine revelation was completed through the apostles, especially through Paul, in a practical sense it also needs to be completed through us today. This means that as we contact people, we must progressively, continually, and gradually preach the word in full. To preach the word in full, or to fully preach the word, is to complete the word. Among so many Christians today there is surely a great need for such a completing of the word....How many of them know God's purpose in saving them? Very few. In Christianity the word of God has been preached, but it has not been preached in full. The preaching of today's Christianity has not completed the word of God. Hence, there is an urgent need for this completion.

In Colossians 1:29 Paul said that he labored, "struggling according to His operation which operates in me in power." Paul labored and struggled for the completion of the word of God. The Greek word indicates that he was wrestling, engaging in combat, for this completion. We can frankly testify that we also are wrestling for the completion of the revelation given to Paul. Apparently in the Lord's ministry we are working; actually we are fighting against religion with its tradition. We need to be clear, however, that our wrestling is not against blood and flesh, but against the evil powers in the heavenlies, against the gates of Hades that seek to destroy the church. As we struggle and fight, our burden, our stewardship, is to complete the word of God. What we are ministering today is the completion of the divine revelation given to Paul.

We need to point out again and again that this revelation concerns Christ as the embodiment of God and the church as the expression of Christ. Although there are a great many Christian activities in this country, there is hardly any completing of the word of God. Who is bearing the burden to declare that Christ the Savior is the life-giving Spirit imparting the divine life into us? Who is discharging the burden to tell the Lord's people that they should be the living Body to express Christ on the proper ground in each locality? We in the Lord's recovery must take up the responsibility for this. The goal of the Lord's recovery is the completion of the word of God. I hope that many brothers will rise up to fulfill this ministry.

Without the completion of the word of God, God's purpose cannot be fulfilled, and Christ cannot obtain His bride or come with His kingdom. We need to experience Christ as the all-inclusive, life-giving Spirit and stand with the church on the proper ground. No matter how much we are opposed and attacked, we must stand with the church and experience Christ in our daily life. (*Life-study of Colossians*, pp. 94, 110-111)

Further Reading: Life-study of Colossians, msg. 13

Enlightenment and inspiration: _____

_____

_____

_____

Morning Nourishment

Col. **Whom we announce, admonishing every man and**
1:28-29 **teaching every man in all wisdom that we may**
present every man full-grown in Christ; for which
also I labor, struggling according to His operation
which operates in me in power.
Eph. **And what is the surpassing greatness of His power**
1:19-20 **toward us who believe, according to the operation**
of the might of His strength, which He caused to
operate in Christ in raising Him from the dead and
seating Him at His right hand in the heavenlies.

I believe that the words "for which" [at the beginning of
Colossians 1:29] refer to the matter of presenting every man
full-grown in Christ. For such a presentation Paul labored, struggled, fought, and wrestled. Paul's struggling, however, was according to Christ's operation within him....This operating is His
energizing. As He energizes us from within, we need to labor in
cooperation with His operating.

The operation of Christ operates "in power."...This power is no
doubt the power of the resurrection life (Phil. 3:10), which operates within the apostle and all the believers (Eph. 1:19; 3:7, 20).
By such an inward operating power of life Christ operates within
us....God's resurrection power accomplishes the spiritual things
for the church within our being. Paul labored, struggled, wrestled,
and fought according to this resurrection power. By means of
the operation in this power he carried out his ministry to present
every saint full-grown in Christ.

May our eyes be opened to see that the goal of our work and
ministry must be to minister Christ to others so that they may
grow with the measure of Christ, who is the mystery of God's
economy. (*Life-study of Colossians,* pp. 119-120)

Today's Reading

Paul's ministry was to impart Christ to others so that they
may be perfect and complete by maturing in Christ unto full
growth [Col. 1:28]. However, many Christian workers today do

not have any concept of presenting every man full-grown in Christ. The goal of their work is something other than this. But we must have the same goal that Paul had.

If we would present others full-grown in Christ, we must minister Christ to them as the portion of the saints (1:12). The Christ we minister must be the all-inclusive One, the centrality and universality of God's economy (1:15, 18-19, 27; 2:4, 9, 16-17; 3:4, 11). If we do not experience Christ in a full way, we shall find it difficult to minister Christ to others. For example, if we do not experience living by Christ, we cannot help anyone else to live by Christ. But if in our daily living we live Christ, grow Christ, and produce Christ, we shall spontaneously infuse Christ into others as we contact them. The more we take Christ as our life and our person, the more we shall be able to minister Christ to others. Having become those who experience Christ and live by Him, we shall influence others to do the same. We need to enjoy Christ as our good land, labor on Him, live in Him, walk in Him, and have our being in Him. If we are such persons, we shall transfuse into others the very Christ whom we experience and by whom we live. In the Lord's recovery what we need is not simply more labor to bring others into the church life. We need to minister the riches of Christ into others so that they may grow and mature. For this we ourselves need to experience more of Christ as the portion of the saints.

Secondly, to present every man full-grown in Christ, we need to minister the unsearchable riches of Christ for the building up of the church to fulfill God's eternal purpose (Eph. 3:8-11). It is possible to be what everyone would consider a good brother or sister, but still be short of the riches of Christ. In my contact with saints as I have traveled, I have met many who lacked the riches of Christ in their daily living, although everyone would consider them very good brothers and sisters. May the Lord awaken within us the aspiration to be rich in Christ. (*Life-study of Colossians*, pp. 129-131)

Further Reading: Life-study of Colossians, msgs. 14, 16

Enlightenment and inspiration: _____

_____

_____

_____

Morning Nourishment

Col. **Of which I became a minister according to the**
1:25-27 **stewardship of God, which was given to me for you,**
to complete the word of God, the mystery which has
been hidden from the ages and from the genera-
tions but now has been manifested to His saints; to
whom God willed to make known what are the
riches of the glory of this mystery among the Gen-
tiles, which is Christ in you, the hope of glory.
Eph. **But holding to truth in love, we may grow up into**
4:15 **Him in all things, who is the Head, Christ.**

We present others full-grown in Christ by completing the
Word of God with the full revelation of Christ and the church (Col.
1:25-27). To present others mature in Christ we must help them
to have the completion of the Word of God concerning Christ as
the mystery of God and the church as the mystery of Christ. However, if we consider our situation, we shall realize that not many of
us are able to complete the Word in this way. For this reason I am
burdened that we would be stirred up to pursue the Lord. We
need to hunger and thirst after Him, to pursue Him until we are
filled with His riches. We need to pray, "Lord Jesus, we don't want
to be indifferent or lukewarm. We long to be absolute with You
and to seek You to the uttermost." If we pursue the Lord in such a
way, we shall see more regarding Christ and the church. But if we
continue to be short of the riches of Christ, we shall not have in
our own experience the completion of the Word of God. Hence,
there is the desperate need for us to pray and to labor on Christ
for the completing of the Word of God concerning Christ and the
church. (*Life-study of Colossians,* pp. 131-132)

Today's Reading

We need to minister Christ as the mystery of God, that is, as
the embodiment of God (Col. 2:2, 9). We need to share with others
from our experience how Christ is the embodiment of the Triune
God. We need to be able to testify how we daily experience Christ
as the Father, Son, and Spirit. Because we have Christ, we also

have the Father. Because we are in Christ, we are also in the Spirit. The Spirit who moves within us actually is Christ Himself. Day by day we should be one spirit with the Lord and experience His being one with us (1 Cor. 6:17). More and more our experience must be that in every aspect of our daily living, wherever we may be, we are one spirit with the Lord. This should not be a doctrine or theory; it must be our practical Christian living.

Concerning my ministry, I often pray like this: "Lord, give me the grace to be one spirit with You as I speak. Lord, I pray that You will speak in my speaking. I believe, Lord, that You are one Spirit with me. But I ask that as I minister the Word I shall be one spirit with You." Whatever impact this ministry has comes from such a oneness with the Lord.

The Lord is the embodiment of the Triune God. This means that all the riches of the Father are embodied in the Son. Furthermore, the Son is realized in a full way as the Spirit, who is now one spirit with us. As Paul says in 1 Corinthians 6:17, "He who is joined to the Lord is one spirit." The matter of being one spirit with the Lord should not be a mere doctrine to us. On the contrary, it must be our daily, practical experience. In our experience we must know what it is to be one spirit with the Lord, who is the embodiment of the Triune God. If we experience Christ as the embodiment of God, we shall be able to minister Christ to others for their nourishment and enrichment. As we minister Christ to others in this way, they will grow in Him. Growth comes by eating. If others feed on the Christ we minister to them as the mystery of God, they will be perfected and mature in Christ.

We need to minister Christ as life to His members so that they may live by Him and grow with Him unto maturity. Colossians 3:4 says that Christ is our life, and in John 6:57; 14:19; and Galatians 2:20 we see that we need to live by Him. Then we shall grow with Him unto maturity (Eph. 4:15, 13). (*Life-study of Colossians*, pp. 132-133, 136)

Further Reading: Life-study of Colossians, msg. 16

Enlightenment and inspiration: _____

_____

_____

_____

Morning Nourishment

Col. For I want you to know how great a struggle I have
2:1-2 for you and *for* those in Laodicea, even all who
      have not seen my face in the flesh, that their hearts
      may be comforted, they being knit together in love
      and unto all the riches of the full assurance of un-
      derstanding, unto the full knowledge of the mys-
      tery of God, Christ.
Mark "And you shall love the Lord your God from your
12:30 whole heart and from your whole soul and from
      your whole mind and from your whole strength."

Only after their hearts had been comforted could the
Colossians receive the revelation concerning Christ. Because this
matter is so important, this book emphasizes the heart instead of
the spirit. We cannot present others full-grown in Christ unless
their hearts have been comforted. If their hearts have not been
cherished, they will not be able to receive anything we minister to
them concerning Christ. Therefore, the first step in presenting
others full-grown in Christ is to comfort their hearts unto all the
riches of the full assurance of understanding. Especially the leading ones should look to the Lord for the grace to be able to comfort
all the distracted, dissatisfied, and disappointed hearts. When the
hearts of the saints have been comforted, it will be easy for us to
minister the riches of Christ to them. But if the saints have problems in their hearts, they will have trouble with their minds. The
only way to solve the problems in the mind is for the hearts to be
adjusted through the Lord's cherishing. This is a crucial lesson for
us all to learn. (*Life-study of Colossians,* pp. 142-143)

Today's Reading

In Colossians 2:2 Paul goes on to speak of all the riches of the
full assurance of understanding. The comforting of the heart must
have a result. In this case the result is having all the riches of the
full assurance of understanding. We need to have such an assurance, for example, concerning the ground of the church. Some
saints claim to know the church ground and to be committed to it.

However, they are actually quite wishy-washy and have no certainty related to the ground of the church. They have faith, but they do not have the certainty which gives us full assurance.

If we would have all the riches of the full assurance of understanding concerning Christ as the mystery of God, every part of our being must be exercised....Certain ones were with us for years. While they were with us, they praised the Lord for His recovery and declared that they were absolutely for the church life. But they eventually turned against the recovery and even condemned it. The reason for such a change is that they never had a thorough exercise concerning the Lord's recovery and never received the full assurance of understanding regarding it.

How much we need to be exercised to know Christ as the mystery of God! We should be able to say, "Lord Jesus, apart from You I have no heart for anything. Lord, my mind, will, and emotion are absolutely for You. I know what I believe, and I know what I am doing in Your recovery. I am willing to lay down my life for You. If I had ten lives, I would give every one of them for the recovery. Every fiber of my being, Lord, is for You." If you exercise your whole being in this way, you will have the full assurance of understanding. You will not have any doubt about what you are doing or about the way you are taking. You will have the kind of assurance martyrs have when they lay down their lives for the Lord.

I wish to emphasize again and again that such riches only come through the exercise of our inner being. In particular, we need to exercise our understanding in studying the Bible. Do not study the Word in a superficial way, and do not take things for granted. Instead, exercise yourself over every phrase, sometimes even over every word....We need to inquire of the Lord and dig into the Word until we have the riches of the full assurance of understanding. To know Christ as the embodiment of God requires such an exercise of our being. (*Life-study of Colossians*, pp. 146-150)

Further Reading: Life-study of Colossians, msgs. 17-18

Enlightenment and inspiration: _____

_____

_____

_____

Hymns, #912

1   Christ to minister is service
        Both to God and others too,
     Christ, the surplus, e'er supplying,
        Off'ring Him as service true.

        Christ to minister is service
           Both to God and others too,
        Christ, the surplus, e'er supplying,
           Off'ring Him as service true.

2   As the Israelites did offer
        From the surplus of their land,
     Thus some produce reaped of Jesus
        Must be in our serving hand.

3   We on Christ, as land, must labor,
        Harvest Him for all our fare;
     Tasting Him to overflowing,
        Christ with others we may share.

4   Holding Christ, as members growing,
        Each his function must observe;
     Christ receiving, Christ partaking,
        To His Body Christ we serve.

5   Fellowship and testimony,
        Ministry and worship too,
     In all helps and ministrations
        Christ is all our service true.

Composition for prophecy with main point and
sub-points: _____

_____

_____

_____

_____

_____

_____

_____

_____

_____

_____

_____

_____

_____

_____

_____

_____

_____

_____

_____

_____

_____

_____

_____

_____

_____

_____

_____

_____

_____

_____

_____

_____

_____

_____

_____

_____

The All-inclusive Christ—
the Mystery of God's Economy
and the Mystery of God

Scripture Reading: Col. 1:25-27; 2:2-3; 1:15-19; 4:3; Eph. 3:3-4

Day 1
&
Day 2

I. **The all-inclusive Christ who indwells us is the mystery of God's economy (Col. 1:26-27):**
   A. God's New Testament economy is like a great wheel, having Christ as its every part—He is the hub (the center), the spokes (the support), and the rim (the circumference) of the divine economy (Ezek. 1:15; Col. 1:17b, 18b):
      1. God's intention in His economy is to work Christ Himself into His chosen people so that Christ may be all and in all (3:10-11; Gal. 1:16a; 2:20; 4:19).
      2. Christ is the mystery, the secret, the crucial focus, of the divine economy; this means that the secret of the dispensing of the Triune God into God's chosen people is Christ Himself (Col. 1:25-28, 17b, 18b; 2:9).
      3. Christ is the Head of the Body (1:18) and the Body of the Head (1 Cor. 12:12); He is all the members and in all the members of the new man (Col. 3:10-11).
   B. The mystery hidden from the ages and from the generations has been made manifest to the saints; this mystery is the all-inclusive Christ as the indwelling hope of glory (1:26-27):
      1. The hope of our calling (Eph. 1:18b; 4:4b) is the hope of glory, which is the transfiguration of our body and the manifestation of the sons of God (Rom. 8:19, 23-25, 30; Phil. 3:21).
      2. The Christ who dwells within us is the mystery full of glory, with countless riches; we are being strengthened into our inner man according to the riches of God's glory, which

are wrought into us for our beautification
and return to God with us for His glorification (Eph. 3:16-21).

3. Christ as the mystery of God's economy is
indwelling us as the hope of glory to be
wrought into us day by day for our transformation from glory to glory unto the full expression of God (2 Cor. 3:18; Rev. 21:10-11).

Day 3 II. **The all-inclusive Christ is the mystery of God
(Col. 2:2):**

A. As the mystery of God, the all-inclusive Christ is
the history of God; the whole "story" of God is in
Christ and is Christ (John 1:14; 1 Cor. 15:45b;
Rev. 4:5).

B. As the mystery of God, the all-inclusive Christ is
the definition, explanation, and expression of
God—the Word of God; in Him are hidden all the
treasures of wisdom and knowledge (John 1:1;
Rev. 19:13; Col. 2:2-3).

C. As the mystery of God, the all-inclusive Christ is
the Firstborn of all creation (Col. 1:15; John 1:14;
Isa. 9:6):

1. Christ as God is the Creator (Heb. 1:10);
however, as man, sharing the created blood
and flesh (2:14a), He is part of the creation.

2. Before the foundation of the world, even before anything was created, God had foreor-
dained that Christ become a created man in
order to accomplish His purpose; hence, in
God's plan and in His eternal view, Christ is
the first one created—He is the Firstborn of
all creation, the Head of all the created ones
(Col. 1:15; Micah 5:2; 1 Pet. 1:20; Rev. 13:8).

Day 4   3. The creation was created in Christ, through
Christ, and unto Christ (Col. 1:16):

a. All things were created in Christ, in the
power of His person; all creation bears
the characteristics of His intrinsic power
(Rom. 1:20).

Day 5

    b. All things were created through Christ as the active instrument through which the creation of all things was accomplished in sequence (John 1:3; Heb. 11:3; Rom. 4:17).

    c. All things were created unto Christ as the end of all creation for His possession (cf. Acts 2:36).

4. Christ is before all things, and all things cohere in Him as the holding center and hub of the universe (Col. 1:17).

5. God's intention in His creation is to use the things of creation to illustrate the all-inclusive Christ; the entire universe came into existence for the purpose of describing Him as the image of the invisible God (v. 15).

D. As the mystery of God, the all-inclusive Christ is the Firstborn from the dead (v. 18):

1. As the Son of God, Christ has passed through two births; the first birth was His incarnation for our judicial redemption, and the second birth was His resurrection for our organic salvation (John 1:14; Acts 13:33; Rom. 1:3-4; 8:29).

2. As the eternally preexistent One, He is our Creator for our existence, as the Firstborn of all creation, He is our Redeemer for our redemption, and as the Firstborn from the dead, He is the life-giving Spirit for our deification (Heb. 2:10-11; cf. Rev. 22:1).

3. Christ is the first in resurrection as the Head of the Body; as such, He has the first place in the church, God's new creation (2 Cor. 5:17; Gal. 6:15).

4. Christ fully expresses the Triune God because He is the Firstborn of both creations, the One through whom both the old creation and the new creation came into being;

the full expression of the rich being of God, in both creation and the church, dwells in Christ (Col. 1:15, 18-19).

Day 6

E. As the mystery of God, the all-inclusive Christ is the embodiment of God; from the time that Christ became incarnate, clothed with a human body, the fullness of the Godhead began to dwell in Him in a bodily way; and in His glorified body now and forever it dwells (2:9; Phil. 3:21; John 20:27-29).

F. As the mystery of God, the all-inclusive Christ is the life-giving Spirit dwelling in our spirit to be one spirit with us; as the life-giving Spirit mingled with our spirit, He is our life and our person (1 Cor. 15:45b; 2 Tim. 4:22; 1 Cor. 6:17; Col. 3:4; Eph. 3:16-17).

G. As the mystery of God, the all-inclusive Christ is the constituent of His Body, the church, which is the mystery of Christ; not only Christ Himself as the Head but also the church as the Body are the manifestation of God in the flesh, the great mystery of godliness (Col. 4:3; Eph. 3:3-4; 5:32; 1 Tim. 3:15-16a; 4:7b).

H. As the mystery of God, the all-inclusive Christ has the first place in all things—in the old creation and the new creation (Col. 1:18b), in the Christian life and experience (Rev. 2:4; 2 Cor. 5:14-15; Gal. 2:20), and in the Christian work and messages (Eph. 2:10; 1 Cor. 2:2; 2 Cor. 4:5).

Morning Nourishment

Col. Of which I became a minister according to the stew-
1:25-27 ardship of God, which was given to me for you, to
complete the word of God, the mystery which has
been hidden from the ages and from the generations
but now has been manifested to His saints; to whom
God willed to make known what are the riches of the
glory of this mystery among the Gentiles, which is
Christ in you, the hope of glory.

3:10-11 And have put on the new man, which is being renewed
unto full knowledge according to the image of Him
who created him, where there cannot be Greek and
Jew, circumcision and uncircumcision, barbarian,
Scythian, slave, free man, but Christ is all and in all.

According to Colossians 3:10-11, in the new man Christ is all and in all. This means that He is all the members of the new man and in all the members.

We may wonder how the church as the Body of Christ can be Christ and how Christ can be all the members of the new man. In our experience, this depends upon who lives. If we live alone by ourselves, we are not Christ. If we live Christ, letting Christ live in us, then we live in Him, and we are Christ. I have seen some wives who really lived their husbands. They did things according to the index of their husbands' eyes. When they lived in such a way, they were their husbands because they lived their husbands. If the church lives Christ, the church is Christ. If we all live Christ, we are Christ. The Christian life should be like this. (*Messages to the Full-time Trainees in Fall 1990*, p. 142)

Today's Reading

[Now] we come to the mystery of God's economy, the mystery that is actually Christ Himself. In Colossians 1:25 Paul speaks of the stewardship of God. The Greek word rendered stewardship, *oikonomia*, may also be rendered economy or administration. The stewardship is the economy, and God's economy is His dispensing. God's intention in His economy is to dispense Himself—the

Father, the Son, and the Spirit—into His chosen people.

Christ is the mystery, the secret, and the crucial focus of the divine economy. This means that the secret of the dispensing of the Triune God into God's chosen people is Christ Himself. Christ is the focal point of God's dispensing. God's dispensing is altogether related to Christ and focused on Him.

Today we focus our attention upon Christ as the mystery of God and upon the church as the mystery of Christ. As the mystery of God, the all-inclusive Christ is the embodiment of God and also the life-giving Spirit. As the mystery of Christ, the church is the Body of Christ, His fullness, and the new man to be the full expression of Christ as well. This is the mystery that has been made manifest to the saints.

The word "whom" at the beginning of verse 27 refers to the saints mentioned in the preceding verse. To us God has willed to make known the riches of the glory of this mystery. This mystery, which is Christ in us as the hope of glory, is made known among the Gentiles. The word "which" in verse 27 refers to the mystery. This mystery full of glory among the Gentiles is Christ in us. Christ in us is mysterious and glorious as well.

Let us now pay closer attention to the riches of the glory of the mystery spoken of in verse 27. The riches of this mystery among the nations are the riches of all that Christ is to the Gentile believers (Eph. 3:8)....These riches include the divine life, the divine nature, the anointing, and the all-inclusive Spirit. Other aspects of the riches are righteousness, justification, holiness, sanctification, transformation, glorification, comfort, and the divine Presence. It is impossible to list all the riches. They are beyond counting. These are the riches of the unique glory, the glory that is ours because we are sons and heirs of God, partners of Christ, and priests and kings. The key to the riches of glory is Christ Himself. (*Life-study of Colossians*, pp. 113, 115-116)

Further Reading: Messages to the Full-time Trainees in Fall 1990,
    ch. 18; *Life-study of Colossians,* msgs. 14-15, 35

Enlightenment and inspiration: _____

_____

_____

Morning Nourishment

Col. To whom God willed to make known what are the
1:27 riches of the glory of this mystery among the Gentiles, which is Christ in you, the hope of glory.
Eph. That He would grant you, according to the riches
3:16-17 of His glory, to be strengthened with power
through His Spirit into the inner man, that Christ
may make His home in your hearts through faith...
Rom. And those whom He predestinated, these He also
8:30 called; and those whom He called, these He also
justified; and those whom He justified, these He
also glorified.

As believers in Christ, we know the riches of the glory of this
mystery. We cannot exhaust the items of the riches of such a glory.
All the blessings in the Bible are included in the riches of this
glory, which is our portion. This glory is the glory of the mystery
among the nations, and this mystery is Christ in us. The Christ
who dwells within us is the mystery full of glory, with countless
riches. This is the key point in the book of Colossians.

Those in Colossae, however, had lost the vision of this mystery
and had become distracted by philosophy, observances, ordinances, and practices. They had been defrauded and carried away
as spoil from their prize, the enjoyment of the all-inclusive Christ.
Like the Colossians, today's Christians have also lost the vision of
the glory of Christ as the mystery of God's economy. The vast ma-
jority of genuine Christians have been distracted and carried
away to things other than Christ Himself. Because the Colossians
had been distracted, Paul wrote to say that the mystery hidden
from the ages and from the generations has been made manifest
to the saints. This mystery is the all-inclusive Christ who indwells us. Because we have the One who is all in all, we have no
need to turn to philosophies, ordinances, observances, and practices. How I look to the Lord that we all may be brought back to
this mystery! Let us forget everything other than Christ and care
only for Him. Christ, the mystery among the Gentiles, has a glory
filled with riches. (*Life-study of Colossians,* p. 117)

Today's Reading

In Colossians 1:27 Paul says that Christ in us is the hope of glory. Christ is the mystery which is full of glory now. This glory will be manifested to its fullest extent when Christ returns to glorify His saints (Rom. 8:30). Hence, it is a hope, the hope of glory. Christ Himself is also this hope of glory.

Today we may live in Christ, by Christ, and with Christ. We may live Him, grow Him, and produce Him. At the same time, He is our hope of glory. If we see the vision that the all-inclusive Christ who indwells us is our hope of glory, our living will be revolutionized. We shall say, "Lord, from now on I won't care for anything other than You....I don't care for religion, philosophy, or the elements of the world. Lord, I care only for You as the embodiment of God and as the life-giving Spirit in my spirit. Because You are so real, living, and practical in my spirit, I can live by You and with You. Lord, my only desire is to experience You in this way."

Eventually, the New Testament charges us to walk according to the mingled spirit (Gal. 5:16, 25; Rom. 8:4). We need to walk according to the Christ who is the very glory filled with riches. Oh, may we all see this vision! Once we have seen this vision, it will control every aspect of our daily walk.

If we see this vision, we shall also realize how much Christians today have been distracted to things other than Christ. They may pay their attention to good things, scriptural things, fundamental things, even spiritual things. Nevertheless, these things are not Christ Himself. It is crucial that we see the Christ who is the mystery hidden from eternity but now made manifest to the saints in the New Testament age. God has willed to make known among the Gentiles the riches of the glory of this mystery, which is Christ in us as the hope of glory. This mystery is the key to our Christian life and also to the church life. (*Life-study of Colossians*, pp. 117-118)

Further Reading: Life-study of Colossians, msg. 14; The Experience of Christ in Galatians, Ephesians, Philippians, and Colossians, ch. 1

Enlightenment and inspiration: _____

_____

_____

_____

Morning Nourishment

Col. **That their hearts may be comforted, they being**
2:2 **knit together in love and unto all the riches of the**
full assurance of understanding, unto the full
knowledge of the mystery of God, Christ.

1:15 **Who is the image of the invisible God, the First-**
born of all creation.

Heb. **...The children have shared in blood and flesh, He**
2:14 **also Himself in like manner partook of the same...**

Rev. **...The book of life of the Lamb who was slain from**
13:8 **the foundation of the world.**

God is a mystery....God is infinite and eternal, without beginning or ending. According to His good pleasure, He created the heavens and the earth and all the billions of items in the universe. Therefore, God accomplished the work of creation....Christ is not only God Himself, but is also God's history. God's history refers to the process through which He has passed so that He may come into man and that man may be brought into Him.

Today the processed Triune God is the Spirit. At the time of John 7:39, the Spirit was not yet, because Jesus had not yet been glorified. He had not yet passed through death and entered into resurrection. Now that Christ has passed through death and has entered into resurrection, the Spirit is here. This Spirit is Christ, and Christ is the story of God, the mystery of God. As the story of God, Christ is the processed God, God processed to become the all-inclusive Spirit, who now dwells in our spirit and is one with our spirit. (*Life-study of Colossians,* pp. 412-413)

Today's Reading

In Colossians 1:15 Paul goes on to say that Christ is the First-born of all creation. This means that in creation Christ is the first. Christ as God is the Creator. However, as man, sharing the created blood and flesh (Heb. 2:14), He is part of the creation. "Firstborn of all creation" refers to Christ's preeminence in all creation, since from this verse through verse 18 the apostle stresses the first place of Christ in all things. This verse reveals that Christ is not only the Creator, but also the first among all created things, the first among all creatures.

Some insist that Christ is only the Creator, not a creature. But the Bible reveals that Christ is both the Creator and a creature, for He is both God and man. As God, Christ is the Creator, but as man, He is a creature. How could He have flesh, blood, and bones if He were not a creature? Did not Christ become a man? Did He not take on a body with flesh, blood, and bones? Certainly He did. Those who oppose this teaching are short of knowledge. Actually, they are heretical, because they do not believe that Christ truly became a man. Rather, they believe only that He is God, and such a belief is heresy. Our Christ is God, has always been God, and always will be God. But through incarnation He became a man. Otherwise He could not have been arrested, tried, and crucified; and He could not have shed His blood on the cross for our sins. Praise the Lord for the truth that our Christ is both God and man!

Some may wonder how Christ could be the Firstborn of all creation since He was born less than two thousand years ago, not at the very beginning of creation. If we would understand this properly, we need to realize that with God there is no time element.

According to our sense of time, Christ was born in Bethlehem approximately two thousand years ago. But in the eyes of God, the Lord Jesus was born before the foundation of the world. If He was slain from the foundation of the world [Rev. 13:8], certainly He must have been born before then. Therefore, according to God's perspective in eternity, Christ was born in eternity past.... According to God's viewpoint, Christ has always been the first of all creatures. God foresaw the day that Christ would be born in a manger in Bethlehem. Because Christ is the first among the creatures, we can say that as the all-inclusive One He is both the Creator and part of creation. (*Life-study of Colossians,* pp. 66-68)

Further Reading: Life-study of Colossians, msgs. 8, 47; *Concerning the Person of Christ*

Enlightenment and inspiration: _____

_____

_____

_____

Morning Nourishment

Col.   Who is the image of the invisible God, the First-
1:15-17   born of all creation, because in Him all things were
created, in the heavens and on the earth, the visible and the invisible, whether thrones or lordships
or rulers or authorities; all things have been created through Him and unto Him. And He is before
all things, and all things cohere in Him.

Actually, all the positive things in the universe may be used to portray what Christ is to us.

God's intention in His creation is to use the things of creation to illustrate the all-inclusive Christ. The entire universe came into existence for the purpose of describing Him. For example, if vines had not been created, the Lord Jesus could not have used a vine to describe Himself. If there were no foxes or birds, Christ could not have compared His situation in His ministry to that of foxes with their holes and birds with their roosts. Even the pasture was created so that the Lord could use it as an illustration of Himself. Furthermore, many different kinds of persons, even a moneylender and a thief, are used to describe Christ. Because the universe with the billions of things and persons in it was created for the purpose of describing Christ, He, in revealing Himself to His disciples, could easily find in any environment something or someone to serve as an illustration of Himself. The whole universe is a picture of Christ. If we see this, we shall realize how rich, profound, unlimited, and unsearchable Christ is. Truly He is everything to us! (*The Conclusion of the New Testament*, p. 522)

Today's Reading

The King James Version of Colossians 1:16 says that all things have been created for Him. It is better to render the Greek "unto Him." "For Him" is objective, but "unto Him" is subjective. All things have been created in Christ, through Christ, and, ultimately, unto Christ. These expressions indicate that Christ has a subjective relationship to creation. Creation is not simply for Him; it is also unto Him. This means that it consummates in Him. The three prepositions in, through, and unto were used by Paul to point out the subjective relationship of Christ to creation. Creation took place in the power of Christ's person, through Him as the active instrument, and unto Him as its consummation. Such a relationship is altogether subjective. Because of His subjective relationship to creation, Christ expresses God in creation. Creation expresses the characteristics of Christ who is the image of the invisible God.

In verse 17 Paul goes on to say, "All things cohere in Him." This means that all things exist together by Christ as the holding center. For creation to subsist in Christ is a further indication that Christ is subjectively related to creation.

It is important to differentiate between the words exist, consist, and cohere. Colossians 1:17 does not say that all things exist in Christ or consist in Him; it says that all things cohere in Him. To exist is to be, to consist is to be composed or constituted, and to cohere is to hold together for existence. Imagine a wheel with its rim, spokes, and hub. All the spokes are held together in the hub. The only way for the spokes to cohere is to be held together at the hub in the center of the wheel. This illustrates Christ's relationship to creation with respect to the fact that all things cohere in Himself.

We have pointed out that all things came into being in Christ, through Christ, and unto Christ. Nothing should be regarded as separate from Him. All things were made in the intrinsic power of Christ's person, through Him as the active instrument, and unto Him as the consummate goal. Furthermore, all things cohere, are held together, in Him as the hub. Because all things were created in Christ, through Christ, and unto Christ and because all things cohere in Christ, God can be expressed in creation through Christ who is the image of the invisible God. (*Life-study of Colossians,* pp. 81-83)

Further Reading: Life-study of Colossians, msg. 10; *The Conclusion of the New Testament,* msg. 48

Enlightenment and inspiration: _____

_____

_____

_____

Morning Nourishment

Col.
1:18   And He is the Head of the Body, the church; He is the beginning, the Firstborn from the dead, that He Himself might have the first place in all things.

Rev.
2:4   But I have *one thing* against you, that you have left your first love.

2 Cor.
5:14-15   For the love of Christ constrains us because we have judged this, that One died for all, therefore all died; and He died for all that those who live may no longer live to themselves but to Him who died for them and has been raised.

Life and experience are inward matters, while the work and messages are outward matters. Whether it be inward matters or outward matters, we should allow Christ to have the first place in all things.

Christ should have the first place in our work. "Good works,…that we would walk in them" (Eph. 2:10). "Good works" are just Christ. The goal of God's work is Christ, and we should walk in this work. All believers, no matter what profession they hold, are doing the work of God and should walk in God's good works. To serve God and to work for God are two vastly different matters. Many work for God but do not serve God. Whether or not a work is of faithfulness depends upon the intent, motive, and purpose and if the goal is for Christ. In doing God's work, although there is suffering, there is also joy; although there is difficulty, there is also comfort. There is also the attraction to God's work. We often work because of our interest, not because of Christ. Many times men run to and fro to work for a name for themselves. They have worked, but they have not served God. God's work from eternity to eternity has always been with the view that His Son would have the first place in all things. Therefore, our work should also be for Christ. (Watchman Nee, *God's Overcomers,* pp. 35-37)

Today's Reading

If God does not purify our intent and motive, we cannot

receive God's blessing. We work not for sinners but for Christ. How successful our work is depends on how much Christ is in it. We should allow the Holy Spirit to discern our intention right from the beginning, to see if it belongs to the spirit or to the soul, and to see if it belongs to this side or to that side. Our work should not be for our own increase, our own group, or our own message; rather, we should work for Christ. As long as God gains something, we should rejoice. When we see God gaining something, even if it is not through our hands, we should be happy for it. We are not saving our message but saving sinners; we are not here to gain our own heart but Christ's heart. When things go our way and we gain something, it means that the Lord gains nothing and nothing goes His way. If we would take God's gain as our satisfaction, we would not be proud or jealous. Many times we seek God's glory as well as our own glory. God saves men for Christ, not for us. Paul planted, and Apollos watered. It was not accomplished by one person, lest anyone would say, "I am of Paul," or "I am of Apollos." All the things concerning the work are for Christ, not for the worker. We are the loaves in the Lord's hand. When people eat the loaves, they thank the one who gives them the loaves; they do not thank the loaves, which are we. The work from its beginning to its end is all for Christ, not for us. We should be satisfied with the work allotted to us by the Lord and with the position the Lord arranged for us. We should not be "in another man's rule" (2 Cor. 10:16). We like very much to leave our own lot to tread on another's lot. The question is not whether we can do it or know how to do it, but whether God has commanded it. Sisters should stand in the sisters' position (1 Cor. 14:34-35). Sisters should not be teachers, making judgments concerning God's word (1 Tim. 2:12). In all the work, we should let Christ have the first place. (Watchman Nee, *God's Overcomers,* pp. 36-37)

Further Reading: Life-study of Colossians, msgs. 9, 13, 18; *God's Overcomers,* ch. 2

Enlightenment and inspiration: _____

_____

_____

_____

Morning Nourishment

Col. And He is the Head of the Body, the church; He is
1:18 the beginning, the Firstborn from the dead, that He
      Himself might have the first place in all things.
1 Cor. For I did not determine to know anything among
2:2   you except Jesus Christ, and this One crucified.
2 Cor. For we do not preach ourselves but Christ Jesus as
4:5   Lord, and ourselves as your slaves for Jesus' sake.

God has accomplished two creations, the old creation and the new creation. The old creation includes heaven, earth, mankind, and millions of different items. The new creation is the church, the Body of Christ. Colossians 1:15-17 unveil Christ as the first in the original creation, as the One who has the preeminence among all creatures. Verse 18 shows that Christ is the first in resurrection as the Head of the Body. He is the One who has the first place in the church.

The first creation came into being through the speaking of God. In the words of Romans 4:17, God called the things not being as being. The new creation, on the contrary, came into being through resurrection, through the death and resurrection of the old creation. In this new creation, the church, Christ is the Firstborn from the dead.

As the Son of God, Christ took two extraordinary steps. Firstly, He took the step of incarnation to become a man for the accomplishment of redemption and for the termination of the old creation. Secondly, in resurrection He became the life-giving Spirit in order to regenerate us to produce the church, God's new creation. (*Life-study of Colossians*, pp. 71, 74)

Today's Reading

Christ should also have the first place in our messages. We "preach ... Christ Jesus as Lord" (2 Cor. 4:5). "For I did not determine to know anything among you except Jesus Christ, and this One crucified" (1 Cor. 2:2). Christ is the center of God's plan and the center of God's goal. The cross is the center of God's work. The work of the cross is to accomplish God's goal. The cross works to eliminate all that issues from the flesh in order that Christ may have the first place. Our central message should not be the dispensations, the prophecies, the types, the kingdom, baptism, forsaking denominations, speaking in tongues, keeping the Sabbath, or holiness, etc. Our central message should be Christ. The centrality of God is Christ. Therefore, we should take Him as the center.

All the truths in the Bible are related like a wheel with spokes and a hub, having Christ as the center. We are not neglecting the truths outside the center; rather, we need to link these truths with the center. Concerning any truth we should know two things: (1) we should know about this truth, and (2) we should know how this truth relates to the center. We should pay attention to the center. Of course, this does not mean we do not speak of other truths....It is only after a person has consecrated himself and received Christ as his Lord that we can speak to him the truths concerning his building up. In our work we should continually draw people back to the center and let them see that "Christ is Lord." We cannot do this work in an objective way. We ourselves must be the first to be broken by God and allow Christ to have the first place in us, before we can lead others to receive Christ as Lord and allow Christ to have the first place in them. We must live out a life of giving Christ the first place before we can spread this message. Our message is just our person. We should allow Christ to have the first place in the small things in our daily life before we can preach the message of the centrality of Christ. I only wish that every one of us would give the Lord Jesus His place on the throne! If the will of God is to be accomplished, what does it matter if I am put in the dust? The Lord's "well done" surpasses all the praises of the world. The smiling face of heaven surpasses all the angry faces of the earth. The comfort of heaven surpasses the tears of the earth. The hidden manna is enjoyed in eternity. May the Lord bless His word that He would gain us and others also. (Watchman Nee, *God's Overcomers,* pp. 37-38)

Further Reading: God's Overcomers, ch. 2

Enlightenment and inspiration: _____

_____

_____

_____

Hymns, #948

1   Myst'ry hid from ages now revealed to me,
     'Tis the Christ of God's reality.
     He embodies God, and He is life to me,
     And the glory of my hope He'll be.

          Glory, glory, Christ is life in me!
            Glory, glory, what a hope is He!
          Now within my spirit He's the mystery!
            Then the glory He will be to me.

2   In my spirit He regenerated me,
     In my soul He's now transforming me.
     He will change my body like unto His own,
     Wholly making me the same as He.

3   Now in life and nature He is one with me;
     Then in Him, the glory, I will be;
     I'll enjoy His presence for eternity
     With Him in complete conformity.

Composition for prophecy with main point and sub-points: _____

_____
_____
_____
_____
_____
_____
_____
_____
_____
_____
_____
_____
_____
_____
_____
_____
_____
_____
_____
_____
_____
_____
_____
_____
_____
_____
_____
_____
_____
_____
_____
_____
_____
_____
_____
_____
_____
_____
_____

The Cross of Christ—
the Unique Way in God's Economy and
the Center of God's Government

Scripture Reading: Col. 1:20-22; 2:11-15; 3:5a

Day 1
&
Day 2

I. **In His economy God gives us one person and one way; the one person is the all-inclusive, extensive, preeminent Christ, and the one way is the cross (1 Cor. 2:2; Phil. 2:5-11; Gal. 6:14):**

A. We not only have Christ, the unique person, who is versus all things; we also have the cross, the unique way, which is versus all ways (Col. 1:20).

B. The way God has ordained, uplifted, and honored is the cross of Christ (Gal. 6:14).

C. The one person—Christ—is the center of the universe, and the one way—the cross—is the center of God's government (1 Cor. 2:2; 1:17-18, 23; Gal. 6:14):

1. God governs everything by the cross and deals with everything by the cross (Col. 1:20; 2:14-15).

2. By the cross God has dealt with all the negative things in the universe, and He is still governing everything through the cross (Eph. 2:14-16).

3. In order to progress spiritually, we need to pass through the cross; until we come to the New Jerusalem, we need to pass through the cross day by day in our walk with the Lord (Matt. 10:38; 16:24; Luke 14:27).

4. In order to have the proper church life, we need to experience the cross; if we have a daily life of passing through the cross, there will be oneness and harmony both in the church life and in the family life (Col. 3:12-15).

Day 3 II. **If we have a clear understanding of the fact that the enemy of God, in a subtle way, utilizes culture to replace Christ, we will realize that the only way for us to take is the way of the cross (Gal. 6:14; 1 Cor. 2:2):**

A. The book of Colossians teaches us that in the church life Christ must be all and in all; everything that is not Christ must go to the cross (1:18; 3:10-11).

B. Through the cross we need to become nothing, to have nothing, and to be able to do nothing; otherwise, what we are, what we have, and what we can do will become a substitute for Christ (1 Cor. 1:17-18, 23).

C. For those who are willing to take the cross, the cross is not a narrow way but a highway (Luke 9:23).

III. **In the book of Colossians we see a clear vision of the cross as God's way in His administration (1:20-22; 2:11-15):**

A. "Through Him to reconcile all things to Himself, having made peace through the blood of His cross—through Him, whether the things on the earth or the things in the heavens" (1:20):

1. *Through Him* means through Christ as the active instrument through which the reconciliation was accomplished (v. 20a).

2. *All things* refers not only to human beings but also to all creatures, which were created in Christ and now subsist, cohere, in Him (vv. 16-17) and are reconciled to God through Him.

3. To reconcile all things to Himself is to make peace with Himself for all things; this was accomplished through the blood of the cross of Christ.

4. Because of the rebellion of Satan, the archangel, and the angels who followed him, the heavens were contaminated; therefore, not only

things on the earth but also things in the heavens needed to be reconciled to God (v. 20b).

5. Because we were sinners, we needed redemption, and because we were also enemies of God, we needed reconciliation (vv. 14, 21-22).

Day 4

B. "Wiping out the handwriting in ordinances, which was against us, which was contrary to us; and He has taken it out of the way, nailing it to the cross" (2:14):

1. *Ordinances* refers to the ordinances of the ceremonial law with its rituals, which are the forms or ways of living and worship (Eph. 2:15).

2. *Nailing it to the cross* means to abolish the law of the commandments in ordinances.

C. "Stripping off the rulers and the authorities, He made a display of them openly, triumphing over them in it" (Col. 2:15):

1. This verse portrays the fighting that took place at the time of Christ's crucifixion.

2. Activities involving Christ, God, and the evil angelic rulers and authorities were brought to a focus on the cross; thus, the cross became God's eternal, central, and unique way (vv. 14-15).

3. By His crucifixion Christ labored to accomplish redemption, and God the Father was working to judge sin and nail the law to the cross (v. 14).

4. At the same time, the evil rulers and authorities were busy in their attempt to frustrate the work of God and Christ, pressing in close to God and Christ; thus, a warfare was raging at the cross.

5. God openly made a display of the evil angelic rulers and authorities on the cross and triumphed over them in it, putting them to shame (v. 15).

Day 5

D. "In Him also you were circumcised with a circumcision not made with hands, in the putting off of the body of the flesh, in the circumcision of Christ" (v. 11):

   1. This is spiritual circumcision, the circumcision of Christ, referring to the proper baptism, which puts off the body of the flesh by the effectual virtue of the death of Christ (Phil. 3:3).

   2. The circumcision that is the putting off of the body of the flesh was not made with hands; it was accomplished by the death of Christ, and it is applied, executed, and carried out by the powerful Spirit (Rom. 8:13).

Day 6

E. "Put to death therefore your members which are on the earth" (Col. 3:5a):

   1. This is based on the fact that we have been crucified with Christ and baptized into His death (Gal. 2:20; Rom. 6:3, 6).

   2. Christ accomplished the all-inclusive crucifixion; now we apply it to our lustful flesh.

   3. We execute Christ's death upon our sinful members by crucifying them, by faith, through the power of the Spirit (Rom. 8:13); this corresponds with Galatians 5:24.

Morning Nourishment

Col. If you died with Christ from the elements of the
2:20-22 world, why, as living in the world, do you subject
yourselves to ordinances: Do not handle, nor taste,
nor touch, (*regarding* things which are all to perish when used) according to the commandments
and teachings of men?

1 Cor. For I did not determine to know anything among
2:2 you except Jesus Christ, and this One crucified.

In His economy God gives us one person and one way. The
one person is the preeminent, all-inclusive Christ, and the one
way is the cross. As the all-inclusive One, Christ is everything to
us. He is God, man, and the reality of every positive thing in the
universe. God has given us this marvelous person to be our salvation. The one person, Christ, is the center of the universe; and
the one way, the cross, is the center of God's government. God
governs everything by the cross and deals with everything by
the cross. Therefore, just as Christ is the focal point of the universe, so the cross is the center of God's government. (*Life-study
of Colossians,* p. 211)

Today's Reading

In this book Paul points out to the Colossians that nothing should become a substitute for Christ. Christ should not be
replaced by ordinances, observances, mysticism, or philosophy.
Christ is everything and must not be replaced by anything. In
the previous message we covered the matter of Christ versus
mysticism. In Colossians mysticism includes Gnosticism and
asceticism. Christ is versus all manner of isms. He is versus every kind of replacement and substitute.

All the positive things in the universe are shadows of
Christ....Since Christ is the substance of all the shadows, we
should not allow the shadows to be a substitute for the One who
is the body, the reality. How foolish to take shadows in place of
the reality!...The all-inclusive Christ is everything to us. God's
intention is not to give us thousands of items; it is simply to give

us one person, the all-inclusive Christ.

Midway through chapter two, Paul begins to show us that the cross is God's unique way. God's way is not asceticism. It is not to humble ourselves, to abase ourselves, or to treat ourselves severely. The one way is the way of the cross. By the cross God has dealt with all the negative things in the universe. Furthermore, God is still governing everything through the cross. Therefore, we have one person and one way; that is, we have Christ and the cross.

As those who have the one person and the one way, we do not need regulations....When we go to bed at night,...we should pass through the cross. This means that no matter what we have done during the day or what has happened to us, the cross takes care of everything. Suppose in the afternoon you are made unhappy in some way by your wife or husband. At bedtime you need to apply the cross to your feeling of unhappiness. If you do this, the feeling of unhappiness will disappear. This indicates that our way is the cross, not asceticism or any severe treatment of the self. Realizing that we have already died in Christ, we should go to bed at night with a consciousness of the cross. If we practice going to bed through the cross, lying down with the realization that we have died in Christ, the next morning we shall wake up in resurrection as a new person. We not only have Christ, the unique person who is versus all things; we also have the cross, the unique way, which is versus all other ways.

Because we have Christ and the cross, there is no place for self-imposed humility. There is no need for us to train ourselves to be humble. I have observed, both in the Orient and in the West, that the most proud people are those who have learned to practice a form of humility. We need not learn such practices. Rather, we should simply take the unique way of the cross. (*Life-study of Colossians,* pp. 211-212, 214-215)

Further Reading: Life-study of Colossians, msg. 26; *The Economy of God,* ch. 1

Enlightenment and inspiration: _____

_____

_____

Morning Nourishment

Gal.   But far be it from me to boast except in the cross of
6:14   our Lord Jesus Christ, through whom the world
       has been crucified to me and I to the world.
Matt. And he who does not take his cross and follow after
10:38 Me is not worthy of Me.
Luke   Whoever does not carry his own cross and come
14:27 after Me cannot be My disciple.

Driving down the street can be a reminder of the way of the cross. As we drive, we come to many intersections....Every intersection is a cross....Some of these crosses may be large and others may be small, but they are all crosses. Only by passing through many crosses can we get to our destination. Speaking of spiritual experience, we also must pass through many crosses before we can reach the New Jerusalem. Just as we cannot travel very far geographically without crossing an intersection, so we cannot progress spiritually without passing through the cross. Only when we arrive at the New Jerusalem shall we cease to pass through the cross, for by that time all the negative things will have been eliminated. Until...[then], we need to pass through the cross day by day in our walk with the Lord.

I can testify that it is a healthy spiritual practice to pass through the cross every night when we go to bed. By applying the cross at the end of each day, I rest very well during the night. At bedtime we need to apply the cross to every problem and to every negative, natural, or sinful thing. We may pray, "Lord, I want all these things to pass through the cross. I do not want to go to sleep with any natural, sinful, negative, or worldly element that has not been dealt with. When I go to bed, Lord, I want to be a person who has been crossed out." We need to be those who pass through one cross after another. I encourage you to daily pass through the intersection of the cross. (*Life-study of Colossians,* pp. 215-216)

Today's Reading

Because we have Christ as the unique person and the cross as the unique way, we do not need asceticism. Furthermore, we do not even need to make up our minds with respect to certain things. Such a practice does not work. What we need to do is simply lie down through the cross at night, have a restful sleep, and then rise up in the morning in resurrection. Praise the Lord that the experience of Christ's death is versus asceticism!

Apart from God's one way, we should have no ordinances and no particular ways or practices. The way God has ordained, uplifted, and honored is the cross of Christ. The cross is our only way. Do you know what can solve the problem of quarreling between husband and wife? It can be solved only by the cross. In the same principle, only the cross can enable the leading ones in a locality to be one and in perfect harmony. We all need to pass through the cross. If we do not experience the cross, we cannot have the proper church life. All the saints must learn to daily pass through the cross. By passing through all manner of crosses, large and small, we shall have oneness and harmony in the church life.

In the church life it is possible to have oneness without harmony. In order to have a sweet harmonious oneness, we all must daily pass through the cross. Do not argue that you are right and that others are wrong. The more you dispute in this way, the less you pass through the cross. To repeat, the way to our destination is through the intersection of the cross. Do not avoid any cross. On the contrary, pass through all the crosses you encounter in the Christian life, in the family life, and in the church life. In married life and in the church life in particular, you need to pass through the cross daily, even hourly. In Ephesians 4 Paul exhorts us not to allow the sun to go down on our anger. This means that we should let go of our anger by passing through the cross. If we have a daily life of passing through the cross, there will be harmony both in the family life and in the church life. Praise the Lord for Christ and the cross! God has given us one person—the all-inclusive Christ— and one way—the cross. (*Life-study of Colossians,* pp. 216-218)

Further Reading: Life-study of Colossians, msg. 26; *God's New Testament Economy,* ch. 3

Enlightenment and inspiration: _____

_____

_____

_____

Morning Nourishment

Col. Beware that no one carries you off as spoil through
2:8 his philosophy and empty deceit, according to the
   tradition of men, according to the elements of the
   world, and not according to Christ.

16 Let no one therefore judge you...

18 Let no one defraud you by judging you unworthy of
   your prize, in self-chosen lowliness and the worship
   of the angels, dwelling on the things which he has
   seen, vainly puffed up by his mind set on the flesh.

1 Cor. But we preach Christ crucified, to Jews a stum-
1:23 bling block, and to Gentiles foolishness.

Luke ...If anyone wants to come after Me, let him deny
9:23 himself and take up his cross daily and follow Me.

According to the economy of God's salvation, the cross is God's central way in the universe. However, most Christians see little of the cross in relation to the spiritual world. For the most part, Christians appreciate the physical aspect of the cross, the aspect that can be observed with human eyes. But in Colossians 2:14 and 15 there is a window through which we can see into the spiritual side of the cross of Christ. When Christ was on the cross, He was not only suffering; He was working to accomplish redemption by bearing our sins and by doing the Father's will. God was also working, wiping out the handwriting in ordinances by nailing it to the cross. As we have pointed out, the evil angelic rulers and authorities were busy also, having come to interfere with what God and Christ were doing. But God stripped them off, triumphed over them in the cross, and put them to an open shame. Of course, on the physical side, the Roman soldiers and the Jewish religionists were also very active. Because all this activity was brought to a focus on the cross, the cross became God's eternal, central, and unique way. (*Life-study of Colossians,* pp. 212-213)

Today's Reading

The main point in the Epistle of Colossians is the fact that in the eyes of God nothing counts except Christ. This fact excludes both good things and bad things, both sinful things and cultured things. In particular, it eliminates all the good aspects of culture. We have pointed out again and again that the enemy of God utilizes culture to replace Christ. This is offensive to God. If Satan cannot corrupt us with evil things, God knows that he will try to use the good aspects of culture to replace Christ. Among today's Christians, where can you find a group of believers with whom you can sense nothing but Christ? Among the various Christian groups we see many good points. However, these good things are not the person of Christ Himself, but something that has replaced Him in a subtle way....If we have a clear view of the situation among Christians today, we shall realize that the background of the book of Colossians exactly corresponds to today's situation. This book was written for us, not only for the saints at Colossae.

If we have a clear understanding of the background of this Epistle, we shall realize that the only way for us to take is the way of the cross. The cross is both a narrow way and a highway. For those not willing to take the cross, the cross is a narrow way. But for those who are willing to take this way, the cross becomes a highway. In the church we all should be nothing and nobody. This was Paul's attitude when he said that we have died and have been buried. To lay hold of this, we need revelation. Whatever we are, whatever we have, and whatever we do can become a substitute for Christ. The better we are or the more capable we are of doing things, the more Christ may be replaced in our experience. Through the cross, we need to become nothing, to have nothing, and to be able to do nothing. Otherwise, what we are, what we have, or what we can do will become a substitute for Christ. Then in our Christian life Christ will not be all in all. The book of Colossians teaches us that in the church life Christ must be all and in all. Everything that is not Christ must go. (*Life-study of Colossians*, pp. 6-7)

Further Reading: Life-study of Colossians, msgs. 1, 9, 26

Enlightenment and inspiration: _____

_____

_____

_____

Morning Nourishment

Col. **Wiping out the handwriting in ordinances, which**
2:14-15 **was against us, which was contrary to us; and He has**
taken it out of the way, nailing it to the cross. Strip-
ping off the rulers and the authorities, He made a
display *of them* **openly, triumphing over them in it.**
Eph. **Abolishing in His flesh the law of the command-**
2:15 **ments in ordinances, that He might create the two in**
Himself into one new man, *so* **making peace.**

Colossians 2:15 portrays the fighting that took place at the
time of Christ's crucifixion. Evil men had put Christ on the cross.
By His crucifixion Christ labored to accomplish redemption. God
the Father was also working to judge sin and to nail the law to the
cross. At the same time, the rulers and authorities were busy in
the attempt to frustrate the work of God and Christ. The refer-
ence to triumph in verse 15 implies fighting. It indicates that a
war was raging. While Christ was accomplishing redemption and
God was dealing with the law and with the negative things, the
rulers and authorities came to interfere. They pressed in close to
God and Christ. But at that very juncture, God stripped them off,
triumphed over them, and made a display of them openly, putting
them to an open shame. (*Life-study of Colossians,* p. 191)

Today's Reading

In a very real sense, the cross of Christ is the center of the
universe. After God created the heavens, the earth, and the billions of items in the universe, an archangel rebelled, and many
angels followed him. This archangel became Satan, and his fol-
lowers became the evil rulers, powers, and authorities in the
heavenlies. Eventually, the man created by God fell and became
sinful. The rebellion of the angels and the fall of man put God
into a difficult situation. God's way to deal with this difficulty is
the cross. Firstly, God became a man, thereby putting humanity
on Himself. Then Christ, God incarnate, went to the cross and
was crucified. During the thirty-three and a half years of His
earthly life, Christ walked from the manger to the cross. When

He was crucified, many things took place. On the cross God judged sin and the sinful old man. Through the cross, our sinful nature was terminated. At the very time God was judging sin and sinful man, He also nailed the law to the cross. When God was nailing the law to the cross, the evil angels also were present and very active. But, according to verse 15, God stripped them off through the cross.

We have pointed out that, according to 2:15, God stripped off the rulers and authorities. From what or from where did He strip them off? If we would answer this question, we must see that while Christ was on the cross, God was working. At that time, the cross was the center of the universe. The Savior, sin, Satan, we, and God all were there. God was there judging sin and nailing the law to the cross. As He was doing this, the rulers and authorities gathered around God and Christ. We have pointed out that, according to grammar, the subject of verses 13 through 15 is God. Thus, the He in verse 15 denotes God. God made us alive together with Christ, nailed the ordinances to the cross, stripped off the rulers and authorities, made a display of them openly, and triumphed over them. No doubt, the rulers and authorities had swarmed around Christ as He was being crucified. Both God and Christ were working. Christ's work was His crucifixion, whereas God's work was to judge sin and all the negative things and to nail the law with its ordinances to the cross. The rulers and authorities who had gathered around God and Christ were also working. If they had not pressed in closely, how could God have stripped them off? The words "stripping off" indicate that they were very close, as close as our garments are to our body. By stripping off the rulers and authorities, God made a display of them openly. He openly put them to shame and triumphed over them. What a great matter this is! (*Life-study of Colossians,* pp. 190-191)

Further Reading: Life-study of Colossians, msg. 23; *Life-study of Matthew,* msg. 70

Enlightenment and inspiration: _____

_____

_____

_____

Morning Nourishment

Col. In Him also you were circumcised with a circumci-
2:11 sion not made with hands, in the putting off of the
body of the flesh, in the circumcision of Christ.
Phil. For we are the circumcision, the ones who serve by
3:3 the Spirit of God and boast in Christ Jesus and
have no confidence in the flesh.
Rom. For if you live according to the flesh, you must die,
8:13 but if by the Spirit you put to death the practices of
the body, you will live.

In Colossians 2:11...Paul speaks of a circumcision not made with hands. This certainly is different from that practiced by the Jews, which was carried out with a knife. In addition to that physical circumcision, there is another kind of circumcision, the circumcision in Christ, which is not made with hands. This is spiritual circumcision and refers to the proper baptism, which puts off the body of the flesh by the effectual virtue of the death of Christ. As we shall see, this is versus asceticism. (*Life-study of Colossians,* pp. 181-182)

Today's Reading

The circumcision in Christ involves the death of Christ and the power of the Spirit. When Christ was crucified on the cross, His crucifixion was the genuine, practical, and universal circumcision. His crucifixion cut off all the negative things. These negative things include our flesh, our natural man, and the self. However, along with the death of Christ we need the Spirit as the power. If we have Christ's crucifixion without the Spirit as the power, we shall have no means to apply Christ's crucifixion to us and to execute its effect upon us. The crucifixion of Christ becomes practical and effective by means of the Spirit. By the Spirit as the power, Christ's crucifixion is applied to us. Then under the power of the Spirit, we are circumcised in an actual and practical way. This is the circumcision in Christ, a circumcision not made with hands. It is a circumcision not made with hands because it was accomplished by the death of Christ, and it is applied, executed, and carried out by the powerful Spirit. This is the circumcision we have all received.

In Christ, on the one hand, we have been made full, and, on the other hand, we have been circumcised. Because we have been made full in Him, we are short of nothing. Because we have been circumcised in Him, all the negative things have been removed. Regarding the positive things, we are complete. Regarding the negative things, everything has been cleared up, and we have no problems. Therefore, regarding the positive things, we are not short of anything, and regarding the negative things, we are no longer troubled by anything.

However, we need to exercise faith and not look at ourselves. We must turn our eyes away from our feelings and from our apparent situation. According to our apparent situation, we are short of everything positive and are troubled by everything negative. But according to the facts, we are not in ourselves—we are in Christ. Because we are in Him, we have been made full positively, and we have been circumcised to clear away the negative things.

In verse 11 Paul speaks of "the putting off of the body of the flesh." This means to strip off something, as to strip off clothing. The circumcision that took place by the death of Christ and is applied by the powerful Spirit accomplishes the putting off of the body of the flesh. Our body of flesh was crucified on the cross with Christ and has been put off. Regarding this, we must again exercise our faith and not consider our self and our apparent situation. Let us exercise faith and say, "Amen! The body of the flesh has been put off on the cross and by the powerful Spirit."

This circumcision must be in the circumcision of Christ, not with a circumcision made with hands. The circumcision of Christ is by His crucifixion. Our flesh has been crossed out by His death on the cross. (*Life-study of Colossians,* pp. 182-183)

Further Reading: Life-study of Colossians, msg. 22

__Enlightenment and inspiration:__ _____

_____

_____

Morning Nourishment

Col. Put to death therefore your members which are on
3:5 the earth: fornication, uncleanness, passion, evil
desire, and greediness, which is idolatry.
Rom. Or are you ignorant that all of us who have been
6:3 baptized into Christ Jesus have been baptized into
His death?
6 Knowing this, that our old man has been crucified
with *Him* in order that the body of sin might be annulled, that we should no longer serve sin as slaves.
Gal. But they who are of Christ Jesus have crucified the
5:24 flesh with its passions and its lusts.

In our sinful members [Col. 3:5] is the law of sin, which makes
us captives of sin and causes our corrupted body to become the
body of death (Rom. 7:23-24). Hence, our members, which are sinful, are identified with sinful things, such as fornication, uncleanness, passion, evil desire, and unbridled greedy lust. In Colossians
3:6 Paul points out that because of these things "the wrath of God
is coming upon the sons of disobedience." In verse 7 he goes on to
say that the believers once walked in these things when they
lived in them. (*Life-study of Colossians,* p. 229)

Today's Reading

In Colossians 3:5 Paul charges us to put to death our members which are on the earth. This charge is based upon the fact
that we have been crucified with Christ (Gal. 2:20a) and that
we have been baptized into His death (Rom. 6:3). We execute Christ's death upon our sinful members by crucifying
them, by faith, through the power of the Spirit (Rom. 8:13). This
corresponds to Galatians 5:24. Christ has accomplished the
all-inclusive crucifixion. Now we apply it to our lustful flesh.
This is absolutely different from asceticism.

Christ's all-inclusive death on the cross is applied to us at the
time of baptism. All those who believe in the Lord Jesus should
be baptized. In baptism we not only recognize Christ's death, but
we also apply it to ourselves. Therefore, in baptism we are placed

into the death of Christ and buried.

According to Romans 8:11 and 13, the putting to death of the practices of the body is an action carried out in the power of the Spirit. It is not accomplished by self-effort. Our attempts to put to death the practices of the body are nothing more than asceticism. Although we are not to practice asceticism, we are to put to death the negative things in us by the power of the Holy Spirit. In order to do this, we need to open to the Spirit and allow the Spirit to flow within us. Through the Spirit's flowing, we shall experience the effectiveness of Christ's death. This is not asceticism; it is the operation of the Spirit within us.

A number of saints have read the autobiography of Madame Guyon. This book contains definite traces of asceticism and mysticism, the very things that damaged the church in Colossae. Those who read books written by the mystics must do so with discernment. Although some things in these books are helpful, others are poisonous. Many years ago, we were helped by some of these books. However, we eventually learned that reading such books without discernment can lead seeking Christians into the error of asceticism. Therefore I do not recommend that you read these books without the help of some saints who are more experienced. Even recently, some, especially sisters, have been damaged by them.

We need to be warned concerning asceticism. We should not impose anything on ourselves in an attempt to deal with the lust of the flesh. On the contrary, our practice should be to open ourselves in fellowship with the Lord and allow the Spirit to have a free way to flow within us, and to apply the effectiveness of Christ's all-inclusive death to the negative things in our being. Asceticism is spiritual suicide; in contrast, what we are speaking of is the application of Christ's death through the flowing of the Spirit. (*Life-study of Colossians,* pp. 230-231)

Further Reading: Life-study of Colossians, msg. 28; *The Collected Works of Watchman Nee,* vol. 8, "Circumcision," pp. 203-212

Enlightenment and inspiration: _____

_____

_____

_____

Hymns, #631

1   If I'd know Christ's risen power,
     I must ever love the Cross;
   Life from death alone arises;
     There's no gain except by loss.

      If no death, no life,
        If no death, no life;
      Life from death alone arises;
        If no death, no life.

2   If I'd have Christ formed within me,
     I must breathe my final breath,
   Live within the Cross's shadow,
     Put my soul-life e'er to death.

3   If God thru th' Eternal Spirit
     Nail me ever with the Lord;
   Only then as death is working
     Will His life thru me be poured.

*Composition for prophecy with main point and
sub-points:* _____

_____

_____

_____

_____

_____

_____

_____

_____

_____

_____

_____

_____

_____

_____

_____

_____

_____

_____

_____

_____

_____

_____

_____

_____

_____

_____

_____

_____

_____

_____

_____

_____

_____

_____

_____

Reading Schedule for the Recovery Version of the New Testament with Footnotes

Wk.	Lord's Day	Monday	Tuesday	Wednesday	Thursday	Friday	Saturday
1	Matt 1:1-2	1:3-7	1:8-17	1:18-25	2:1-23	3:1-6	3:7-17
2	4:1-11	4:12-25	5:1-4	5:5-12	5:13-20	5:21-26	5:27-48
3	6:1-8	6:9-18	6:19-34	7:1-12	7:13-29	8:1-13	8:14-22
4	8:23-34	9:1-13	9:14-17	9:18-34	9:35—10:5	10:6-25	10:26-42
5	11:1-15	11:16-30	12:1-14	12:15-32	12:33-42	12:43—13:2	13:3-12
6	13:13-30	13:31-43	13:44-58	14:1-13	14:14-21	14:22-36	15:1-20
7	15:21-31	15:32-39	16:1-12	16:13-20	16:21-28	17:1-13	17:14-27
8	18:1-14	18:15-22	18:23-35	19:1-15	19:16-30	20:1-16	20:17-34
9	21:1-11	21:12-22	21:23-32	21:33-46	22:1-22	22:23-33	22:34-46
10	23:1-12	23:13-39	24:1-14	24:15-31	24:32-51	25:1-13	25:14-30
11	25:31-46	26:1-16	26:17-35	26:36-46	26:47-64	26:65-75	27:1-26
12	27:27-44	27:45-56	27:57—28:15	28:16-20	Mark 1:1	1:2-6	1:7-13
13	1:14-28	1:29-45	2:1-12	2:13-28	3:1-19	3:20-35	4:1-25
14	4:26-41	5:1-20	5:21-43	6:1-29	6:30-56	7:1-23	7:24-37
15	8:1-26	8:27—9:1	9:2-29	9:30-50	10:1-16	10:17-34	10:35-52
16	11:1-16	11:17-33	12:1-27	12:28-44	13:1-13	13:14-37	14:1-26
17	14:27-52	14:53-72	15:1-15	15:16-47	16:1-8	16:9-20	Luke 1:1-4
18	1:5-25	1:26-46	1:47-56	1:57-80	2:1-8	2:9-20	2:21-39
19	2:40-52	3:1-20	3:21-38	4:1-13	4:14-30	4:31-44	5:1-26
20	5:27—6:16	6:17-38	6:39-49	7:1-17	7:18-23	7:24-35	7:36-50
21	8:1-15	8:16-25	8:26-39	8:40-56	9:1-17	9:18-26	9:27-36
22	9:37-50	9:51-62	10:1-11	10:12-24	10:25-37	10:38-42	11:1-13
23	11:14-26	11:27-36	11:37-54	12:1-12	12:13-21	12:22-34	12:35-48
24	12:49-59	13:1-9	13:10-17	13:18-30	13:31—14:6	14:7-14	14:15-24
25	14:25-35	15:1-10	15:11-21	15:22-32	16:1-13	16:14-22	16:23-31
26	17:1-19	17:20-37	18:1-14	18:15-30	18:31-43	19:1-10	19:11-27

Reading Schedule for the Recovery Version of the New Testament with Footnotes

Wk.	Lord's Day	Monday	Tuesday	Wednesday	Thursday	Friday	Saturday
27	Luke 19:28-48	20:1-19	20:20-38	20:39—21:4	21:5-27	21:28-38	22:1-20
28	22:21-38	22:39-54	22:55-71	23:1-43	23:44-56	24:1-12	24:13-35
29	24:36-53	John 1:1-13	1:14-18	1:19-34	1:35-51	2:1-11	2:12-22
30	2:23—3:13	3:14-21	3:22-36	4:1-14	4:15-26	4:27-42	4:43-54
31	5:1-16	5:17-30	5:31-47	6:1-15	6:16-31	6:32-51	6:52-71
32	7:1-9	7:10-24	7:25-36	7:37-52	7:53—8:11	8:12-27	8:28-44
33	8:45-59	9:1-13	9:14-34	9:35—10:9	10:10-30	10:31—11:4	11:5-22
34	11:23-40	11:41-57	12:1-11	12:12-24	12:25-36	12:37-50	13:1-11
35	13:12-30	13:31-38	14:1-6	14:7-20	14:21-31	15:1-11	15:12-27
36	16:1-15	16:16-33	17:1-5	17:6-13	17:14-24	17:25—18:11	18:12-27
37	18:28-40	19:1-16	19:17-30	19:31-42	20:1-13	20:14-18	20:19-22
38	20:23-31	21:1-14	21:15-22	21:23-25	Acts 1:1-8	1:9-14	1:15-26
39	2:1-13	2:14-21	2:22-36	2:37-41	2:42-47	3:1-18	3:19—4:22
40	4:23-37	5:1-16	5:17-32	5:33-42	6:1—7:1	7:2-29	7:30-60
41	8:1-13	8:14-25	8:26-40	9:1-19	9:20-43	10:1-16	10:17-33
42	10:34-48	11:1-18	11:19-30	12:1-25	13:1-12	13:13-43	13:44—14:5
43	14:6-28	15:1-12	15:13-34	15:35—16:5	16:6-18	16:19-40	17:1-18
44	17:19-34	18:1-17	18:18-28	19:1-20	19:21-41	20:1-12	20:13-38
45	21:1-14	21:15-26	21:27-40	22:1-21	22:22-29	22:30—23:11	23:12-15
46	23:16-30	23:31—24:21	24:22—25:5	25:6-27	26:1-13	26:14-32	27:1-26
47	27:27—28:10	28:11-22	28:23-31	Rom 1:1-2	1:3-7	1:8-17	1:18-25
48	1:26—2:10	2:11-29	3:1-20	3:21-31	4:1-12	4:13-25	5:1-11
49	5:12-17	5:18—6:5	6:6-11	6:12-23	7:1-12	7:13-25	8:1-2
50	8:3-6	8:7-13	8:14-25	8:26-39	9:1-18	9:19—10:3	10:4-15
51	10:16—11:10	11:11-22	11:23-36	12:1-3	12:4-21	13:1-14	14:1-12
52	14:13-23	15:1-13	15:14-33	16:1-5	16:6-24	16:25-27	I Cor 1:1-4

Reading Schedule for the Recovery Version of the New Testament with Footnotes

Wk.	Lord's Day	Monday	Tuesday	Wednesday	Thursday	Friday	Saturday
53	☐ I Cor 1:5-9	☐ 1:10-17	☐ 1:18-31	☐ 2:1-5	☐ 2:6-10	☐ 2:11-16	☐ 3:1-9
54	☐ 3:10-13	☐ 3:14-23	☐ 4:1-9	☐ 4:10-21	☐ 5:1-13	☐ 6:1-11	☐ 6:12-20
55	☐ 7:1-16	☐ 7:17-24	☐ 7:25-40	☐ 8:1-13	☐ 9:1-15	☐ 9:16-27	☐ 10:1-4
56	☐ 10:5-13	☐ 10:14-33	☐ 11:1-6	☐ 11:7-16	☐ 11:17-26	☐ 11:27-34	☐ 12:1-11
57	☐ 12:12-22	☐ 12:23-31	☐ 13:1-13	☐ 14:1-12	☐ 14:13-25	☐ 14:26-33	☐ 14:34-40
58	☐ 15:1-19	☐ 15:20-28	☐ 15:29-34	☐ 15:35-49	☐ 15:50-58	☐ 16:1-9	☐ 16:10-24
59	☐ II Cor 1:1-4	☐ 1:5-14	☐ 1:15-22	☐ 1:23—2:11	☐ 2:12-17	☐ 3:1-6	☐ 3:7-11
60	☐ 3:12-18	☐ 4:1-6	☐ 4:7-12	☐ 4:13-18	☐ 5:1-8	☐ 5:9-15	☐ 5:16-21
61	☐ 6:1-13	☐ 6:14—7:4	☐ 7:5-16	☐ 8:1-15	☐ 8:16-24	☐ 9:1-15	☐ 10:1-6
62	☐ 10:7-18	☐ 11:1-15	☐ 11:16-33	☐ 12:1-10	☐ 12:11-21	☐ 13:1-10	☐ 13:11-14
63	☐ Gal 1:1-5	☐ 1:6-14	☐ 1:15-24	☐ 2:1-13	☐ 2:14-21	☐ 3:1-4	☐ 3:5-14
64	☐ 3:15-22	☐ 3:23-29	☐ 4:1-7	☐ 4:8-20	☐ 4:21-31	☐ 5:1-12	☐ 5:13-21
65	☐ 5:22-26	☐ 6:1-10	☐ 6:11-15	☐ 6:16-18	☐ Eph 1:1-3	☐ 1:4-6	☐ 1:7-10
66	☐ 1:11-14	☐ 1:15-18	☐ 1:19-23	☐ 2:1-5	☐ 2:6-10	☐ 2:11-14	☐ 2:15-18
67	☐ 2:19-22	☐ 3:1-7	☐ 3:8-13	☐ 3:14-18	☐ 3:19-21	☐ 4:1-4	☐ 4:5-10
68	☐ 4:11-16	☐ 4:17-24	☐ 4:25-32	☐ 5:1-10	☐ 5:11-21	☐ 5:22-26	☐ 5:27-33
69	☐ 6:1-9	☐ 6:10-14	☐ 6:15-18	☐ 6:19-24	☐ Phil 1:1-7	☐ 1:8-18	☐ 1:19-26
70	☐ 1:27—2:4	☐ 2:5-11	☐ 2:12-16	☐ 2:17-30	☐ 3:1-6	☐ 3:7-11	☐ 3:12-16
71	☐ 3:17-21	☐ 4:1-9	☐ 4:10-23	☐ Col 1:1-8	☐ 1:9-13	☐ 1:14-23	☐ 1:24-29
72	☐ 2:1-7	☐ 2:8-15	☐ 2:16-23	☐ 3:1-4	☐ 3:5-15	☐ 3:16-25	☐ 4:1-18
73	☐ I Thes 1:1-3	☐ 1:4-10	☐ 2:1-12	☐ 2:13—3:5	☐ 3:6-13	☐ 4:1-10	☐ 4:11—5:11
74	☐ 5:12-28	☐ II Thes 1:1-12	☐ 2:1-17	☐ 3:1-18	☐ I Tim 1:1-2	☐ 1:3-4	☐ 1:5-14
75	☐ 1:15-20	☐ 2:1-7	☐ 2:8-15	☐ 3:1-13	☐ 3:14—4:5	☐ 4:6-16	☐ 5:1-25
76	☐ 6:1-10	☐ 6:11-21	☐ II Tim 1:1-10	☐ 1:11-18	☐ 2:1-15	☐ 2:16-26	☐ 3:1-13
77	☐ 3:14—4:8	☐ 4:9-22	☐ Titus 1:1-4	☐ 1:5-16	☐ 2:1-15	☐ 3:1-8	☐ 3:9-15
78	☐ Philem 1:1-11	☐ 1:12-25	☐ Heb 1:1-2	☐ 1:3-5	☐ 1:6-14	☐ 2:1-9	☐ 2:10-18

Reading Schedule for the Recovery Version of the New Testament with Footnotes

Wk.	Lord's Day	Monday	Tuesday	Wednesday	Thursday	Friday	Saturday
79	☐ Heb 3:1-6	☐ 3:7-19	☐ 4:1-9	☐ 4:10-13	☐ 4:14-16	☐ 5:1-10	☐ 5:11—6:3
80	☐ 6:4-8	☐ 6:9-20	☐ 7:1-10	☐ 7:11-28	☐ 8:1-6	☐ 8:7-13	☐ 9:1-4
81	☐ 9:5-14	☐ 9:15-28	☐ 10:1-18	☐ 10:19-28	☐ 10:29-39	☐ 11:1-6	☐ 11:7-19
82	☐ 11:20-31	☐ 11:32-40	☐ 12:1-2	☐ 12:3-13	☐ 12:14-17	☐ 12:18-26	☐ 12:27-29
83	☐ 13:1-7	☐ 13:8-12	☐ 13:13-15	☐ 13:16-25	☐ James 1:1-8	☐ 1:9-18	☐ 1:19-27
84	☐ 2:1-13	☐ 2:14-26	☐ 3:1-18	☐ 4:1-10	☐ 4:11-17	☐ 5:1-12	☐ 5:13-20
85	☐ I Pet 1:1-2	☐ 1:3-4	☐ 1:5	☐ 1:6-9	☐ 1:10-12	☐ 1:13-17	☐ 1:18-25
86	☐ 2:1-3	☐ 2:4-8	☐ 2:9-17	☐ 2:18-25	☐ 3:1-13	☐ 3:14-22	☐ 4:1-6
87	☐ 4:7-16	☐ 4:17-19	☐ 5:1-4	☐ 5:5-9	☐ 5:10-14	☐ II Pet 1:1-2	☐ 1:3-4
88	☐ 1:5-8	☐ 1:9-11	☐ 1:12-18	☐ 1:19-21	☐ 2:1-3	☐ 2:4-11	☐ 2:12-22
89	☐ 3:1-6	☐ 3:7-9	☐ 3:10-12	☐ 3:13-15	☐ 3:16	☐ 3:17-18	☐ I John 1:1-2
90	☐ 1:3-4	☐ 1:5	☐ 1:6	☐ 1:7	☐ 1:8-10	☐ 2:1-2	☐ 2:3-11
91	☐ 2:12-14	☐ 2:15-19	☐ 2:20-23	☐ 2:24-27	☐ 2:28-29	☐ 3:1-5	☐ 3:6-10
92	☐ 3:11-18	☐ 3:19-24	☐ 4:1-6	☐ 4:7-11	☐ 4:12-15	☐ 4:16—5:3	☐ 5:4-13
93	☐ 5:14-17	☐ 5:18-21	☐ II John 1:1-3	☐ 1:4-9	☐ 1:10-13	☐ III John 1:1-6	☐ 1:7-14
94	☐ Jude 1:1-4	☐ 1:5-10	☐ 1:11-19	☐ 1:20-25	☐ Rev 1:1-3	☐ 1:4-6	☐ 1:7-11
95	☐ 1:12-13	☐ 1:14-16	☐ 1:17-20	☐ 2:1-6	☐ 2:7	☐ 2:8-9	☐ 2:10-11
96	☐ 2:12-14	☐ 2:15-17	☐ 2:18-23	☐ 2:24-29	☐ 3:1-3	☐ 3:4-6	☐ 3:7-9
97	☐ 3:10-13	☐ 3:14-18	☐ 3:19-22	☐ 4:1-5	☐ 4:6-7	☐ 4:8-11	☐ 5:1-6
98	☐ 5:7-14	☐ 6:1-8	☐ 6:9-17	☐ 7:1-8	☐ 7:9-17	☐ 8:1-6	☐ 8:7-12
99	☐ 8:13—9:11	☐ 9:12-21	☐ 10:1-4	☐ 10:5-11	☐ 11:1-4	☐ 11:5-14	☐ 11:15-19
100	☐ 12:1-4	☐ 12:5-9	☐ 12:10-18	☐ 13:1-10	☐ 13:11-18	☐ 14:1-5	☐ 14:6-12
101	☐ 14:13-20	☐ 15:1-8	☐ 16:1-12	☐ 16:13-21	☐ 17:1-6	☐ 17:7-18	☐ 18:1-8
102	☐ 18:9—19:4	☐ 19:5-10	☐ 19:11-16	☐ 19:17-21	☐ 20:1-6	☐ 20:7-10	☐ 20:11-15
103	☐ 21:1	☐ 21:2	☐ 21:3-8	☐ 21:9-13	☐ 21:14-18	☐ 21:19-21	☐ 21:22-27
104	☐ 22:1	☐ 22:2	☐ 22:3-11	☐ 22:12-15	☐ 22:16-17	☐ 22:18-21	☐

Week 1 — Day 4 Today's verses	**Week 1 — Day 5** Today's verses	**Week 1 — Day 6** Today's verses
Col. If therefore you were raised together with 3:1 Christ, seek the things which are above, where Christ is, sitting at the right hand of God. 1:27 To whom God willed to make known what are the riches of the glory of this mystery among the Gentiles, which is Christ in you, the hope of glory. 1 Cor. But he who is joined to the Lord is one 6:17 spirit.	Col. When Christ our life is manifested, then 3:4 you also will be manifested with Him in glory. 10-11 And have put on the new man, which is being renewed unto full knowledge according to the image of Him who created him, where there cannot be Greek and Jew, circumcision and uncircumcision, barbarian, Scythian, slave, free man, but Christ is all and in all.	Eph. That Christ may make His home in your 3:17 hearts through faith... Phil. For to me, to live is Christ... 1:21
_____ Date	_____ Date	_____ Date

Week 1 — Day 1 Today's verses	**Week 1 — Day 2** Today's verses	**Week 1 — Day 3** Today's verses
Col. Who is the image of the invisible God, the 1:15 Firstborn of all creation. 18 And He is the Head of the Body, the church; He is the beginning, the Firstborn from the dead, that He Himself might have the first place in all things. Eph. To me...was this grace given to announce 3:8 to the Gentiles the unsearchable riches of Christ as the gospel.	Matt. ...This is My Son, the Beloved, in whom I 17:5 have found My delight. Hear Him! Gal. I am crucified with Christ; and it is no longer 2:20 I _who_ live, but it is Christ _who_ lives in me; and the _life_ which I now live in the flesh I live in faith, the _faith_ of the Son of God... Eph. Unto the economy of the fullness of the 1:10 times, to head up all things in Christ... 3:17 That Christ may make His home in your hearts through faith... Col. To whom God willed to make known what 1:27 are the riches of the glory of this mystery among the Gentiles, which is Christ in you, the hope of glory.	Col. Therefore we also, since the day we heard 1:9 of _it_, do not cease praying and asking on your behalf that you may be filled with the full knowledge of His will in all spiritual wisdom and understanding, 12 Giving thanks to the Father, who has qualified you for a share of the allotted portion of the saints in the light.
_____ Date	_____ Date	_____ Date

Week 2 — Day 4 — Today's verses

Col.
2:6-7 As therefore you have received the Christ, Jesus the Lord, walk in Him, having been rooted and being built up in Him...

11 In Him also you were circumcised with a circumcision not made with hands, in the putting off of the body of the flesh, in the circumcision of Christ.

13 And you, though dead in your offenses and in the uncircumcision of your flesh, He made alive together with Him, having forgiven us all our offenses.

_____
Date

Week 2 — Day 5 — Today's verses

Col.
2:6-10 As therefore you have received the Christ, Jesus the Lord, walk in Him, having been rooted and being built up in Him, and being established in the faith even as you were taught, abounding in thanksgiving. Beware that no one carries you off as spoil through his philosophy and empty deceit, according to the tradition of men, according to the elements of the world, and not according to Christ; for in Him dwells all the fullness of the Godhead bodily, and you have been made full in Him, who is the Head of all rule and authority.

_____
Date

Week 2 — Day 6 — Today's verses

Col.
4:2 Persevere in prayer, watching in it with thanksgiving.

Matt.
14:23 And after He sent the crowds away, He went up to the mountain privately to pray. And when night fell, He was there alone.

6:6 But you, when you pray, enter into your private room, and shut your door and pray to your Father who is in secret; and your Father who sees in secret will repay you.

_____
Date

Week 2 — Day 1 — Today's verses

Col.
1:12 Giving thanks to the Father, who has qualified you for a share of the allotted portion of the saints in the light.

2:6-7 As therefore you have received the Christ, Jesus the Lord, walk in Him, having been rooted and being built up in Him, and being established in the faith even as you were taught, abounding in thanksgiving.

Gal.
3:14 In order that the blessing of Abraham might come to the Gentiles in Christ Jesus, that we might receive the promise of the Spirit through faith.

_____
Date

Week 2 — Day 2 — Today's verses

Psa.
119:105 Your word is a lamp to my feet and a light to my path.

Phil.
2:15 That you may be blameless and guileless, children of God without blemish in the midst of a crooked and perverted generation, among whom you shine as luminaries in the world.

1 Pet.
2:9 But you are a chosen race, a royal priesthood, a holy nation, a people acquired for a possession, so that you may tell out the virtues of Him who has called you out of darkness into His marvelous light.

1 John
1:5 ...God is light and in Him is no darkness at all.

_____
Date

Week 2 — Day 3 — Today's verses

S. S.
4:11 Your lips drip fresh honey, my bride; honey and milk are under your tongue...

Psa.
119:103 How sweet are Your words to my taste! Sweeter than honey to my mouth!

Isa.
50:4 The Lord Jehovah has given me the tongue of the instructed, that I should know how to sustain the weary with a word....

Luke
4:22 And all bore witness to Him and marveled at the words of grace proceeding out of His mouth...

Eph.
4:29 Let no corrupt word proceed out of your mouth, but only that which is good for building up, according to the need, that it may give grace to those who hear.

_____
Date

Week 3 — Day 1

Today's verses

Mark 1:15 …The kingdom of God has drawn near. Repent and believe in the gospel.

Mark 4:26 And He said, So is the kingdom of God: as if a man cast seed on the earth.

Luke 17:20-21 And when He was questioned by the Pharisees as to when the kingdom of God was coming, He answered them and said, The kingdom of God does not come with observation….For behold, the kingdom of God is in the midst of you.

Rom. 14:17 For the kingdom of God is not eating and drinking, but righteousness and peace and joy in the Holy Spirit.

Date _____

Week 3 — Day 2

Today's verses

John 1:12-14 But as many as received Him, to them He gave the authority to become children of God, to those who believe into His name, who were begotten not of blood, nor of the will of the flesh, nor of the will of man, but of God. And the Word became flesh and tabernacled among us (and we beheld His glory, glory as of the only Begotten from the Father), full of grace and reality.

3:3 …Unless one is born anew, he cannot see the kingdom of God.

5 …Unless one is born of water and the Spirit, he cannot enter into the kingdom of God.

Date _____

Week 3 — Day 3

Today's verses

Col. 1:13 Who delivered us out of the authority of darkness and transferred us into the kingdom of the Son of His love.

Acts 26:18 To open their eyes, to turn them from darkness to light and from the authority of Satan to God, that they may receive forgiveness of sins and an inheritance among those who have been sanctified by faith in Me.

Heb. 2:14 Since therefore the children have shared in blood and flesh, He also Himself in like manner partook of the same, that through death He might destroy him who has the might of death, that is, the devil.

Date _____

Week 3 — Day 4

Today's verses

Matt. 16:24 Then Jesus said to His disciples, If anyone wants to come after Me, let him deny himself and take up his cross and follow Me.

Col. 3:5 Put to death therefore your members which are on the earth: fornication, uncleanness, passion, evil desire, and greediness, which is idolatry.

8 But now, you also, put away all these things: wrath, anger, malice, blasphemy, foul abusive language out of your mouth.

Date _____

Week 3 — Day 5

Today's verses

1 John 5:11 And this is the testimony, that God gave to us eternal life and this life is in His Son.

1 Pet. 2:9 But you are a chosen race, a royal priesthood, a holy nation, a people acquired for a possession, so that you may tell out the virtues of Him who has called you out of darkness into His marvelous light.

John 1:18 No one has ever seen God; the only begotten Son, who is in the bosom of the Father, He has declared Him.

Matt. 3:17 …This is My Son, the Beloved, in whom I have found My delight.

Date _____

Week 3 — Day 6

Today's verses

1 John 5:12 He who has the Son has the life; he who does not have the Son of God does not have the life.

Col. 3:4 When Christ our life is manifested, then you also will be manifested with Him in glory.

John 6:57 As the living Father has sent Me and I live because of the Father, so he who eats Me, he also shall live because of Me.

Matt. 3:17 …This is My Son, the Beloved, in whom I have found My delight.

Date _____

Week 4 — Day 1

Today's verses

Col. 1:25 Of which I became a minister according to the stewardship of God, which was given to me for you....

Eph. 3:8-9 To me, less than the least of all saints, was this grace given to announce to the Gentiles the unsearchable riches of Christ as the gospel and to enlighten all *that they may see* what the economy of the mystery is, which throughout the ages has been hidden in God, who created all things.

1 Cor. 9:17 If I do this of my own will, I have a reward; but if not of my own will, I am entrusted with a stewardship.

Date

Week 4 — Day 2

Today's verses

Col. 1:24 I now rejoice in my sufferings on your behalf and fill up on my part that which is lacking of the afflictions of Christ in my flesh for His Body, which is the church.

John 12:24 Truly, truly, I say to you, Unless the grain of wheat falls into the ground and dies, it abides alone; but if it dies, it bears much fruit.

26 If anyone serves Me, let him follow Me...

Phil. 3:10 To know Him and the power of His resurrection and the fellowship of His sufferings, being conformed to His death.

2 Tim. 2:10 Therefore I endure all things for the sake of the chosen ones, that they themselves also may obtain the salvation which is in Christ Jesus with eternal glory.

Date

Week 4 — Day 3

Today's verses

Col. 1:25 Of which I became a minister according to the stewardship of God, which was given to me for you, to complete the word of God.

Acts 20:26-27 Therefore I testify to you on this day that I am clean from the blood of all men, for I did not shrink from declaring to you all the counsel of God.

Eph. 5:32 This mystery is great, but I speak with regard to Christ and the church.

Date

Week 4 — Day 4

Today's verses

Col. 1:28-29 Whom we announce, admonishing every man and teaching every man in all wisdom that we may present every man full-grown in Christ; for which also I labor, struggling according to His operation which operates in me in power.

Eph. 1:19-20 And what is the surpassing greatness of His power toward us who believe, according to the operation of the might of His strength, which He caused to operate in Christ in raising Him from the dead and seating Him at His right hand in the heavenlies.

Date

Week 4 — Day 5

Today's verses

Col. 1:25-27 Of which I became a minister according to the stewardship of God, which was given to me for you, to complete the word of God. the mystery which has been hidden from the ages and from the generations but now has been manifested to His saints; to whom God willed to make known what are the riches of the glory of this mystery among the Gentiles, which is Christ in you, the hope of glory.

Eph. 4:15 But holding to truth in love, we may grow up into Him in all things, who is the Head, Christ.

Date

Week 4 — Day 6

Today's verses

Col. 2:1-2 For I want you to know how great a struggle I have for you and *for* those in Laodicea, even all who have not seen my face in the flesh, that their hearts may be comforted, they being knit together in love and unto all the riches of the full assurance of understanding, unto the full knowledge of the mystery of God, Christ.

Mark 12:30 "And you shall love the Lord your God from your whole heart and from your whole soul and from your whole mind and from your whole strength."

Date

Week 5 — Day 4

Today's verses

Col. 1:15-17 Who is the image of the invisible God, the Firstborn of all creation, because in Him all things were created, in the heavens and on the earth, the visible and the invisible, whether thrones or lordships or rulers or authorities; all things have been created through Him and unto Him. And He is before all things, and all things cohere in Him.

Date

Week 5 — Day 5

Today's verses

Col. 1:18 And He is the Head of the Body, the church; He is the beginning, the Firstborn from the dead, that He Himself might have the first place in all things.

Rev. 2:4 But I have *one thing* against you, that you have left your first love.

2 Cor. 5:14-15 For the love of Christ constrains us because we have judged this, that One died for all, therefore all died; and He died for all that those who live may no longer live to themselves but to Him who died for them and has been raised.

Date

Week 5 — Day 6

Today's verses

Col. 1:18 And He is the Head of the Body, the church; He is the beginning, the Firstborn from the dead, that He Himself might have the first place in all things.

1 Cor. 2:2 For I did not determine to know anything among you except Jesus Christ, and this One crucified.

2 Cor. 4:5 For we do not preach ourselves but Christ Jesus as Lord, and ourselves as your slaves for Jesus' sake.

Date

Week 5 — Day 1

Today's verses

Col. 1:25-27 Of which I became a minister according to the stewardship of God, which was given to me for you, to complete the word of God, the mystery which has been hidden from the ages and from the generations but now has been manifested to His saints; to whom God willed to make known what are the riches of the glory of this mystery among the Gentiles, which is Christ in you, the hope of glory.

3:10-11 And have put on the new man, which is being renewed unto full knowledge according to the image of Him who created him, where there cannot be Greek and Jew, circumcision and uncircumcision, barbarian, Scythian, slave, free man, but Christ is all and in all.

Date

Week 5 — Day 2

Today's verses

Col. 1:27 To whom God willed to make known what are the riches of the glory of this mystery among the Gentiles, which is Christ in you, the hope of glory.

Eph. 3:16-17 That He would grant you, according to the riches of His glory, to be strengthened with power through His Spirit into the inner man, that Christ may make His home in your hearts through faith....

Rom. 8:30 And those whom He predestinated, these He also called; and those whom He called, these He also justified; and those whom He justified, these He also glorified.

Date

Week 5 — Day 3

Today's verses

Col. 2:2 That their hearts may be comforted, they being knit together in love and unto all the riches of the full assurance of understanding, unto the full knowledge of the mystery of God, Christ.

1:15 Who is the image of the invisible God, the Firstborn of all creation.

Heb. 2:14 ...The children have shared in blood and flesh, He also Himself in like manner partook of the same...

Rev. 13:8 ...The book of life of the Lamb who was slain from the foundation of the world.

Date

Week 6 — Day 1 — Today's verses

Col. If you died with Christ from the elements
2:20-22 of the world, why, as living in the world,
do you subject yourselves to ordinances:
Do not handle, nor taste, nor touch, (regarding things which are all to perish
when used) according to the commandments and teachings of men?

1 Cor. For I did not determine to know anything
2:2 among you except Jesus Christ, and this
One crucified.

_____
Date

Week 6 — Day 2 — Today's verses

Gal. But far be it from me to boast except in the
6:14 cross of our Lord Jesus Christ, through
whom the world has been crucified to me
and I to the world.

Matt. And he who does not take his cross and
10:38 follow after Me is not worthy of Me.

Luke Whoever does not carry his own cross
14:27 and come after Me cannot be My disciple.

_____
Date

Week 6 — Day 3 — Today's verses

Col. Beware that no one carries you off as spoil
2:8 through his philosophy and empty deceit,
according to the tradition of men, according to the elements of the world, and not
according to Christ.

16 Let no one therefore judge you...

18 Let no one defraud you by judging you unworthy of your prize, in self-chosen lowliness and the worship of the angels, dwelling
on the things which he has seen, vainly
puffed up by his mind set on the flesh.

Luke ...If anyone wants to come after Me, let him
9:23 deny himself and take up his cross daily
and follow Me.

_____
Date

Week 6 — Day 4 — Today's verses

Col. Wiping out the handwriting in ordi-
2:14-15 nances, which was against us, which was
contrary to us; and He has taken it out of
the way, nailing it to the cross. Stripping
off the rulers and the authorities, He made
a display of them openly, triumphing over
them in it.

Eph. Abolishing in His flesh the law of the
2:15 commandments in ordinances, that He
might create the two in Himself into one
new man, so making peace.

_____
Date

Week 6 — Day 5 — Today's verses

Col. In Him also you were circumcised with a
2:11 circumcision not made with hands, in the
putting off of the body of the flesh, in the
circumcision of Christ.

Phil. For we are the circumcision, the ones
3:3 who serve by the Spirit of God and boast
in Christ Jesus and have no confidence in
the flesh.

Rom. For if you live according to the flesh, you
8:13 must die, but if by the Spirit you put to
death the practices of the body, you will
live.

_____
Date

Week 6 — Day 6 — Today's verses

Col. Put to death therefore your members
3:5 which are on the earth: fornication, uncleanness, passion, evil desire, and
greediness, which is idolatry.

Rom. Or are you ignorant that all of us who
6:3 have been baptized into Christ Jesus have
been baptized into His death?

6 Knowing this, that our old man has been
crucified with Him in order that the body
of sin might be annulled, that we should
no longer serve sin as slaves.

Gal. But they who are of Christ Jesus have cru-
5:24 cified the flesh with its passions and its
lusts.

_____
Date